Life on the
DEATH BEAT

Life on the
DEATH BEAT

A Handbook for Obituary Writers

By Alana Baranick, Jim Sheeler and Stephen Miller

Marion Street Press, Inc.
PO Box 2249, Oak Park, IL 60303
www.marionstreetpress.com

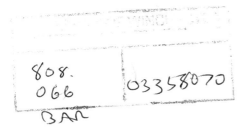
Cover illustration by Mike Meredith

ISBN 1-933338-01-6
Printed in U.S.A.
Printing 10 9 8 7 6 5 4 3 2 1

Marion Street Press, Inc.
PO Box 2249
Oak Park, IL 60303
866-443-7987
www.marionstreetpress.com

Dedicated to obituary writers, obituary readers and the thousands of obituary subjects we wish we had known.

Contents

Foreword

The Art of the Obit

The obituary has earned a place in our culture as an important and distinct literary form. Even the casual reader of the obituary page seems to understand its value. Aficionados of the art of the obituary gain comfort in finding nuggets of historical or genealogical facts in these miniature tales of life. Writers and journalists love finding the well-turned phrase or the special use of language in the obituary.

The art of the obituary is now enjoying a renaissance of sorts. Whereas the obituary of old reflected a traditional attitude toward end of life issues; that is, that certain things are not talked about — death, dying, burials, obituaries — after World War II that attitude began a slow shift to one of viewing the obituary as a story of life rather than a pronouncement of death. In fact, as baby boomers begin to grey, many of them see the obituary as an important part of their family history and, as such, that it should be written with their input if possible. Certainly, they are not as restrained as their parents or grandparents when it comes to the content of the obituary for family members or for themselves.

Perhaps one of the most visible turning points in this obituary renaissance was a result of the tragedies of September 11, 2001. Those shocking and untimely deaths called for obituaries of a different kind. These were not people at the end of their lives and careers; they were vibrant thirty-forty-fifty somethings who were in the prime of their lives. Those who tried to rescue them were healthy, young public servants. These deaths cried out for a unique kind of obituary which would share the vitality, hopes and dreams of these lives stopped short.

That special kind of obituary vignette emerged in media in the places where the events unfolded so cruelly: New York City, Washington, D.C., Boston.

The New York Times, The Washington Post and the Boston Globe crafted a new style of obituary vignette which was written not for the purpose giving funeral or memorial service information — because in many cases that information would not be available due to the fact that the individuals were not found or identified for some time. Instead, the vignettes became a way for families to share their love and grief in a positive and immediate way. Portraits of Grief by The New York Times writers is an example of this obituary genre which has influenced style and substance of obituaries to come.

You are about to enter the realm of three very talented obituarists. They approach the obituary with all the tools of the experienced, demanding — yet sensitive — journalist. Each has a different style of writing and interviewing.

Each has a unique skill for assembling research and molding it into the ultimate short story in a way that leads the reader on with great interest.

Each is skilled technically and has the curiosity of an investigative detective who finds himself on an important case. These are the qualities that have earned these writers professional recognition among their peers.

As founder of the International Association of Obituarists, I have been fortunate not only to study the content, form and language of obituaries but also to know the writers themselves. Alana Baranick, Stephen Miller and Jim Sheeler graciously have shared their professional talent with their colleagues at the annual Great Obituary Writers' International Conferences for several years.

Each of the three journalists whose work you are about to read is a story unto himself. Baranick practices her craft at the Plain Dealer in Cleveland, Ohio. Miller is the obits editor for the New York Sun. Sheeler is an obits specialist who writes for Denver's Rocky Mountain News.

As diverse as they are in personality and writing style, they have at least two important qualities in common: (1) they have an unswerving dedication to accuracy and excellence and (2) they have senses of humor to die for!

Baranick has made it her style to tell the life stories of the good , the bad and the ugly in her obituaries. She is a master of clever understatement and almost always discovers something heretofore unknown about her subjects that makes the reader wish he had known that person. Her obituaries have solved mysteries and uncovered many a strange turn in the life she is revealing.

Foreword

Miller has for years been the driving force behind an obituary website "Good-Bye: The Journal of Contemporary Obituaries." This online e-zine exemplifies the dedication to research and language dexterity that has become the hallmark of Stephen Miller. The site is on hiatus as Miller practices his craft as obits editor for the New York Sun, where his obits shine brightly.

Sheeler has established his own unique style for the obituary. He approaches the work as a "life story" which is written not in the immediate hours following a death but written in the next days or weeks, based on personal interviewing of family and friends. The luxury of in-depth research and contact with the family results in an obituary that is approached as a news story. The result is a mini-biography that is a rare gift for family and community alike. He, of course, also writes stellar obituaries of the traditional style on a daily basis.

Those of us who read the obituary pages daily are very proud of these writers. Those of you who are journalists and practicing obituarists are in for a treat as you read and study "Life On the Death Beat."

CAROLYN MILFORD GILBERT
Founder
International Association of Obituarists
www.ObitPage.com

Introduction

Writing Deadlines

Alana Baranick

Obituaries. A man or a woman lives their entire life. They work and love and dream and laugh and cry. Then they die. And then somebody, who they don't even know, who's never met them once, boils their entire life down to a paragraph or two in a local newspaper.

And that's only if they've achieved something some editor thinks is important. Now, if they're real movers and shakers, they may get two columns. Maybe they get a photo from 1974. And if they've achieved nothing, they get buried at the bottom of the page or ignored completely.

- from the HBO prison series, *Oz*

I am an obituary writer, one of those strangers — or, if you prefer, those strange people — who sum up the lives of people we've never met. I've been writing obituaries for the Plain Dealer in Cleveland, Ohio, since 1992 and at a smaller paper for several years before that.

Like a detective, I interview witnesses, gather evidence and study various records from which I formulate an image of the dearly departed. Often I come away from the experience feeling somewhat like actor Dana Andrews' character in the movie "Laura," a cop who investigates a homicide and ends up wishing he'd had a chance to meet the murder victim.

The stories I write may be splashed across the top of the obit page, possibly with a photo and a two-line headline, or wedged into the bottom corner next to an ad for a monument company and the phone number for the Veterans Administration. On occasion, they may make it to the metro cover or even the front page. Or they may not be printed at all.

As an obituary writer for Ohio's largest daily newspaper, I inform the public when one of its numbers has lost her valiant battle with a devastating illness, walked out of his wheelchair and into the arms of the Lord or, in cold, harsh newspaper terms, died.

Yet the fact of the death is merely the peg on which to hang the story of the life of a fellow human being. Who was this person who just forded the great gulf to the final frontier? How did he use his allotted time? What made her special?

An obituary is an attempt to answer these questions, usually in 500 words or less and on the publisher's deadline. It adds identifying details — age, job, relatives, personality traits — to the announcement of a person's death and funeral arrangements.

Obituaries shouldn't be platforms from which to praise the recently departed without regard to their flaws. Nor should obits indict the deceased for their shortcomings. Like the obituary's more prestigious colleagues — the news stories that dominate the front page and sometimes win Pulitzers for their authors — obit articles should be fair, balanced, accurate and aimed at providing information to the readers.

Obits shape the way future generations perceive the past. Genealogists and scholars use them as the basis for their own versions of history, often without regard to accuracy.

These once-in-a-lifetime stories, handed down from generation to generation, could easily outlive their composers. And yet, obituary writing is among the least respected and least coveted assignments in the newsroom.

As a dissatisfied reporter assigned to obit duty in the movie "Perfect," actor John Travolta tells his editor, "I cannot take this anymore. You've got to get me off the obituary desk. I cannot write another obituary. I mean it."

Fictional obit writers, in books like "Basket Case" and "The Obituary Writer," are often portrayed as unfulfilled and ashamed of their journalistic lot in life. Obituary writing really is a job considered "dead end" by many people, particularly journalists.

It doesn't matter that surveys show obituaries to be among the most widely read and enduring stories in the newspaper. It seems that we obituary writers get no respect. Many editors hand the task to novice reporters as a training exercise, to old-timers as a nudge toward retirement, or to rogue reporters as penance for sins against the publisher.

What fools! Obit duty should be regarded as a reward, not a punishment, and something to be entrusted to the best reporters and writers. The death beat crosses over into all other news beats. The only common thread is that the subject has died. Penning post-mortem profiles demands attention to detail, understanding of the times in which the deceased lived, and the ability to give an accurate report, even though the chief witness is not available to testify.

A well-written and well-researched obit can enlighten readers about contemporary history and a variety of ethnic, religious and socio-economic cultures. It also can provide information about agencies, events and individuals that can help the reader or benefit from the reader's support.

If we're lucky, an obituary will inspire the living to be good to their neighbors, strive for success and keep hope alive.

Stephen Miller of the New York Sun, Jim Sheeler of the Rocky Mountain News and I believe that summing up a life is an awesome responsibility, challenge and privilege. Obit writing exercises all of our journalistic skills, broadens our scope of knowledge, and sharpens our perception of life and death.

In this book, we'll offer guidelines for compiling and researching obits to be printed in a newspaper. We'll also discuss the pros, cons and peculiarities of an obituary writer's life on the death beat. We'll also introduce you to some extraordinary people you'll wish you had known.

A LIFE STORY

Harriet Stansbury Norris, 1910-2003

THE FRUITS OF HER LABOR;

HEAVENLY PLEDGE MET BY SUPPLYING PRODUCE TO SHELTERS

By Alana Baranick, Plain Dealer Reporter

Gourmet fruit baskets took their rightful place in the ranks of traditional floral arrangements at the funeral of a woman known at local soup kitchens as "The Banana Lady."

Harriet Norris, who died Jan. 20 at age 93, put fresh fruit on the breakfast table at St. Herman's House of Hospitality from its inception in the late 1970s until health problems ended her gratis grocery delivery service about 20 years later.

She also made sure that the destitute and disenfranchised at several other shelters had their daily minimum requirement of fruits and vegetables. Her own children certainly did.

"She was famous for trying to get us to eat extra salad by compressing all the ingredients tightly in a big bowl," said her

14

daughter, Mary Ellen Nowel of Morro Bay, Calif.

"Each of us got one of these pre-packed bowls with dinner every night. It never seemed to empty."

Realizing that fresh produce was always in short supply at mission centers, Norris vowed to rectify the situation.

At least once a week, she engaged in lively haggling matches with distributors at the Northern Ohio Food Terminal on the East Side.

She struck deals for 40-pound boxes of appetizing lettuce, tomatoes, apples, and, most often, bananas, which she packed into an ancient Bonneville sedan, dubbed the Market Mobile.

Then she shoehorned herself behind the steering wheel and delivered the goods to hunger centers, thereby keeping her part of the bargain that she had made with God during World War II:

"Bring my husband home from the war alive, and I'll dedicate my life to service."

The Cleveland native, born Harriet Stansbury, was 32 when she married Jim Norris in 1942. Before meeting him on a blind date, she worked as a secretary in Baltimore, took some courses in botany and turned down five marriage proposals. Although she was impressed with Jim's high moral principles, she demanded a good reason he shouldn't become her sixth disappointed suitor.

"When he proposed, he told her he thought they could help save each other's souls," Nowel said. "Who could resist a line like that?"

After her husband returned from combat in the Pacific, Norris began making good on her prayerful promise. She canned peaches, baked cookies and did laundry for elderly neighbors.

She bought dozens of children's shoes at thrift shops for clothing drives at St. Ignatius Church. She had her own sons and daughters clean and polish the footwear, reminding them, "The poor deserve something beautiful." She also took refurbished clothing to Sister Henrietta, the legendary nun who helped the poor in the Hough area.

Norris cherry-picked at supermarkets, often wheeling two carts at a time to collect drastically reduced-in-price, label-less cans that provided culinary mysteries for the homeless and her own household.

The feisty great-grandmother also freely dispensed opinions to the beneficiaries of her goodwill and the folks running the hunger centers. She scolded young ruffians in her path, petitioned city officials to get drug dealers out of the neighborhood and acted as an advocate for nursing home patients.

After Norris' husband retired from Alcoa, he became her cohort in good-deed-doing. While he entertained nursing home residents with his piano playing, she took bouquets to patients who didn't get many visitors. She got the blooms from floral arrangements that had been abandoned by bereaved families at the Walter Martens & Son Funeral Home.

Norris, a longtime member of the Cleveland Hiking Club, kept up the pace into her late 80s, going it alone after her husband's death in 1995.

"When she'd come in and have a cup of tea with me, she'd always tell me a story about her beloved Jim," said Terrie Garr of the West Side Catholic Center.

Norris was buried next to her husband on Jan. 24, their wedding anniversary.

Her children were all there: Nowel, Jean Nagy of Cleveland, David of Rocky River, Philip of Parma and Kathleen DiRusso of Arvada, Colo.

And they donated the fruit baskets from her funeral to St. Herman's.

Chapter 1

Your Basic Obit

ALANA BARANICK

The world would be a better place if most of the people I've written about were still alive.

According to their relatives and associates, most of the recently deceased were giving, caring individuals who would do anything for anybody, always thought of others before themselves and loved family above all else.

They were honest, hard-working, fun-loving, intelligent renaissance people, astute in business, devout in their faith and kind to animals. Each was honest to a fault, had a wonderful sense of humor, and would give you the shirt off his back. They never met a stranger, never complained when they were suffering, and never said an unkind word about anyone.

They were so special and touched so many lives, it's no wonder they will "sorely be missed by all."

Bereaved relatives generally don't understand that an obituary written by a reporter is not the same thing as a eulogy. It is a news story, which in all probability will include the good, the bad and the ugly of a person's life, especially if that person was a public figure.

For an obit writer, it's an awesome responsibility to be entrusted with summing up a person's life, and you get only one shot at it. Even when I believe that I've done a terrific job and have written the obit so well that readers think I personally knew the deceased, I always feel that I could have done better.

An obituary writer, who has to pick and choose only a few out of dozens of possible obit-page subjects, has to ask herself, "Did I choose wisely? Did I miss the story of the century?"

Of course, the movers and shakers are natural candidates for obituary coverage because of their significant contributions to the community, celebrity status and available archival data. The obituary writer can easily compose a mini-biography when the continuing saga of a person's life has been recorded in the newspaper or listed in history books.

Once in a while, a newspaper's top brass will "strongly suggest" that certain obituaries be written. Most of the time these are understandable requests — an obit for a bank chairman, a well-known car dealer, a pioneering medical researcher.

Sometimes the higher-ups want us to write about the mother, brother-in-law or cousin of the bank chairman, car dealer or researcher. If the famous person's relative has no claim to fame of his own, writing the obit can be difficult, but it is not impossible.

I am convinced that every person's life is interesting, although it is not always obvious from what the funeral director or the relatives initially tell us. Some folks are interesting because they are different. Others because they are people with whom we can identify. Their stories are compelling because they represent scores of people with similar backgrounds.

I get plenty of requests to write obits for women who began their teaching careers in one-room schoolhouses. For factory workers who started their own machine tooling businesses in their garages. For veterans of foreign wars and Holocaust survivors. For folks who migrated from West Virginia, Alabama or Puerto Rico to my neck of the woods for job opportunities. And for Yugoslavian or Vietnamese immigrants who fled religious or political persecution in their homelands.

The obit page should be the newspaper's model for celebrating diversity of race, ethnicity, social status and occupation. After all, people from all walks of life die. Obituaries shouldn't be the private domain of old, rich, white men. Seek out black obituary candidates, women, blue-collar workers, and people with disabilities. Your body of work will be more interesting, and you'll learn a lot in the process.

ONE OF THE BIGGEST CHALLENGES for families wishing to get a loved one's final story into a newspaper is sorting through the sundry terms and methods for reporting deaths. Not all newspapers use the same terminology. One newspaper's "obituary" is another publication's "death notice." Some are free. Others are printed for a fee.

The terms and conditions of publication also may vary from one day to the next at a single newspaper, depending on the obit writer, the editor, or the publisher's financial consid- erations. Obit writers, like tour guides, have to be able to lead fam- ilies through the maze.

When I'm contacted by a bereaved relative, I usually ask what funeral home is handling the arrangements. If a local mortuary was in charge, my familiarity with various funeral directors' attitudes and approaches toward reporter- written obituaries usually tells me whether the family needs to take a more aggressive role in the process.

In some cases, I base my evalu- ation of a potential obit on the funeral director's degree of involvement in the obit pitch. If a funeral director calls us about every case that comes through his funeral home, I don't jump to attention unless I'm given some compelling bit of information.

Others, who don't want to get involved, routinely tell bereaved families to contact us themselves. When those funeral directors take time to call us, I know that the deceased was either a prominent person or a friend of the mortician.

Obit Building Blocks

1. Name and age of the deceased.

2. Day, date, place, cause and/or cir- cumstances of death.

3. Place of birth, last city of residence and other places the deceased had called home.

4. Education, military background and work history.

5. Volunteer service, memberships, awards and honors, hobbies and interests.

6. Surviving relatives and where they live; deceased relatives and when they died.

7. Time and place of funeral or memo- rial services.

8. Requests for memorial donations, along with mailing addresses.

9. Name and phone number of funer- al home or cremation society.

10. Phone numbers where family can be reached.

As a professional courtesy, I really do try to accommodate morticians and newspaper colleagues who ask, "Can you do my friend's or relative's obit as a favor to me?" But I can't always. I have to follow our paper's unwritten rules about choosing newsmakers, exceptionally interesting stories and editor-mandated obits first. Often, we grim writers simply do not have sufficient time to complete an obit before deadline. So many obits, so little time.

WHILE THE MANNER IN WHICH DEATHS ARE REPORTED may vary from paper to paper and from obit writer to obit writer, most are built upon the same basic bricks of biographical information and details about the death and funeral arrangements. It's helpful to have a fill-in-the-blanks obit-

Obit Variety

Here are some of the methods newspapers use to report a death.

Reporter-written obituaries. These are news stories printed at the discretion of the editorial staff and at no charge. The stories may contain more or less information than that which was provided by the family. The newspapers are under no obligation to run these or to run them word-for-word as requested by the families. Some papers print every obit that is submitted. Others do not.

Family-placed obituaries. These are stories prepared by the family or funeral director, often printed for a fee. The content may be edited by newspaper personnel.

Death notices. These are classified ads. Families pay to place these, and they're usually printed as submitted. Family-placed obituaries also may fall under this category.

Memorial notices. These are eulogies, poems about heaven, "We miss you" messages and the like, sometimes placed on the anniversary of the deceased's death or birth. These are paid for.

Public service listings. This is a free service, not offered by all newspapers, which offers a line or two that says little more than, "This person has died."

News stories prompted by the circumstances of death. When a person dies tragically — in a traffic or industrial accident, is the victim of a homicide or a casualty of war, or died as the result of some highly contagious disease that may put the community at risk — the death may be addressed in a news story. Reporters sometimes interview relatives to learn more about the deceased, but the story usually doesn't include information about the funeral or surviving relatives.

information form handy to distribute to funeral directors and, upon request, to families.

Review the provided information with the family. Make sure it is accurate, that spellings are correct and that the numbers — ages, dates, etc. — add up. If the informant doesn't know a specific date, try to narrow it down to a particular period of time, such as "the late 1980s," "around 1987" or "nearly 20 years ago."

Watch for unexplained gaps in time. Grandpa may have been a hero in World War II, but what did he do with the rest of his life? What did Uncle Joe do in the 15 years between graduating from college and starting his own company? Why did Cousin Dollie retire so young, and what has she done since then?

A beloved sister may have been an inspiration during her 5-year bout with cancer, but surely she did something besides fight death during her 48 years on the planet. If that is indeed all she ever did, then you have to wonder whether her obit should be written at all. Would readers be interested?

And just because Mom was effectively out of commission with Alzheimer's disease for the last 10 years, don't let the grieving son forget about the vibrant life his mother lived before that. Can you imagine Ronald Reagan's obituary focusing on what he referred to as his "journey into the sunset of my life," instead of his accomplishments as U.S. president, California governor and Hollywood movie star?

Watch out for exaggerations. If some of the information is unreliable, you may not be able to trust the rest of it.

Get specifics about employment. If the deceased "retired from the automobile plant," what automaker did she work for and for how long? Which plant? When did she retire? Did she paint the car chassis, type requisitions for parts, or manage the plant?

If the dearly departed "worked in the food service industry," did he wait tables? Did he fill vending machines with candy and potato chips? Did he manage a steak house or run a chain of delicatessens?

Don't try to make a job sound more prestigious by using euphemisms or exaggerations. Every job is important. A garbage collector performs one of the most important jobs in any city. It's not necessary to call him an "environmental engineer" to elevate his stature. And remember that the executive who oversees a manufacturing company wouldn't have a job if there were no skilled laborers to make his products.

Be mindful of terminology. You don't have to use words like "attorney," "Realtor" or "entrepreneur" just because the bereaved relatives do. Remember, you're a journalist. You can use more appropriate methods to express what the person did for a living.

Use active verbs. Minimize the number of times you use forms of the verb "to be." Instead of writing, "He was an attorney," say, "He specialized in copyright law." The occupation of a woman whom relatives called a "Realtor" becomes more interesting when we tell the reader, "She sold bungalows near the airport to veterans returning from wartime service in the late 1940s." And it's better to explain that the deceased "opened hot dog stands in every major city east of the Mississippi" than to just say that he was an entrepreneur.

Don't feel obliged to include all the information provided by the family or every detail you find in your research. And don't limit yourself. You can add information the family hadn't expected, as long as you know it's true. Focus on that part of the decedent's life that you believe is the most important.

Name dropping should be avoided in an obit most of the time, unless the deceased's connection with the celebrity is paramount to the story. If the dearly departed was Bob Hope's press agent, that would be significant. But if the late loved one was among the thousands of soldiers entertained by the legendary comedian during one of his overseas Christmas shows, forget about it.

I'm sure the bereaved's great-grandma felt really special when she received a letter from the president of the United States congratulating her on the occasion of her 100th birthday. But it's not something that I would consider pertinent to her obituary. Nowadays anyone who reaches the century mark can get greetings from our nation's fearless leader, as long as someone takes time to request it from the White House.

The same can be said of common military medals and commendations. Military service, in peace or war, is a noble endeavor, but announcing that Grandpa was a recipient of the Good Conduct Medal and World War II Victory Medal says nothing more than "He was a World War II veteran." (See Chapter 6 for more information on writing about veterans.)

It's good to gather information about the dearly beloved's jobs, volunteer work, education, military service, political involvement, memberships, honors and hobbies. Those things help us develop an image of that person's life.

But it's not necessary to include all of it. Saying that someone who was past retirement age belonged to the American Association of Retired Persons does not enhance that person's obituary. The same principle applies to various professional memberships. We expect lawyers to be members of bar associations, physicians to belong to medical organizations and engineers to be affiliated with engineering societies.

If the deceased had served as president of a particular professional group, we might mention it, because that generally shows a high level of commitment. In some cases, however, that doesn't work. Being the founder and grand exalted ruler of a two-man club you formed with your brother isn't exactly a major accomplishment. But it might make a colorful anecdote.

Consider the elements that combine for a good story. It's a nice touch to share that a rocket scientist raised prize-winning roses, that a construction worker was known for baking lemon meringue pies or that a petite cosmetologist held a black belt in karate.

Public relations representatives who contact us on behalf of their clients sometimes forget that an obit is not an advertisement for the company with which the deceased or his family was affiliated. If a restaurateur's mother dies, I want to know about Mom. I'm not interested in what's on the menu at her son's restaurant, unless she taught him how to cook it.

One public relations rep for a political candidate offered us obit info for the mother of a campaign worker a couple of weeks before an election. The press release emphasized how the dead woman, who was not a resident of the candidate's district and would not have been able to vote for him, fervently supported his candidacy. Well, I guess that makes sense. Chances are, if he won the election, the deceased's campaign-working child may have landed a government job.

© The Plain Dealer, May 15, 2000

DUANE NAFTZGER
STARTED FROG JUMP IN VALLEY CITY

By Alana Baranick, Plain Dealer Reporter

Liverpool Township — Duane M. Naftzger, 79, helped launch the annual event that earned the unincorporated Liverpool Township hamlet of Valley City the title: "Frog Jump Capital of Ohio." He died Friday at his home in that community.

Since it sprang into the spotlight 38 years ago, the Valley City Frog Jump has become an annual event, growing by leaps and bounds from approximately 135 entries its first year to 575 last year.

It also has become an integral part of the rural Medina County community's folklore. According to the modern-day legend, Mr. Naftzger and his friend Andrew Neff were nursing some double sarsaparillas at a local pub when they came up with the idea of incorporating a frog-jumping contest, like the one made famous by Mark Twain's short story, "The Celebrated Jumping Frog of Calaveras County," in Liverpool Township's sesquicentennial celebration in 1962.

Mr. Naftzger, who served as the announcer for the contest for 25 years before stepping down in 1987, liked to spin colorful frog-related yarns, letting the listener determine where reality ended and myth began.

He regularly told stories about the dueling fire chiefs of the Erhart and Valley City fire departments, who reportedly stooped to measures which, if they were true, would have drawn the ire of animal rights activists.

One of his down-home vignettes was set in the metropolis

23

of Cleveland, where Frog Jump representatives, dressed in costumes of the Twain era, went to publicize their summer ritual. As the story goes, one of them was carrying on his lap under a derby a frog, which he had trained to jump whenever he whistled. When the owner of the frog noticed an attractive young woman walking down Euclid Ave. and emitted a wolf whistle, the well-trained frog jumped out of the open window into the path of an oncoming city bus.

"That was true," said his widow, Marjorie. "They had this frog in a gallon jar, and he did jump out of the jar." Regarding the whistling and the bus, she added, "A lot of this stuff was tongue-in-cheek, but it made good publicity. If he wanted to do something, he went after it. He never did anything half-heartedly."

The history of Liverpool Township "written by this here fella Duane Naftzger" and the rules, records and background of the annual Frog Jump, which next will be held Aug. 13, can be found on the Internet at: http://www.valleycity.org.

Mr. Naftzger was born in York Township and graduated from York High School. In recent years, he was involved with projects of the York Historical Society.

During World War II, he served in the Army in New Guinea and the Philippines.

He had been commander of Medina Veterans of Foreign Wars Post 5137 and of the VFW Medina County Council. He had been a quartermaster of Valley City VFW Post 5563.

For several years, he owned the Naftzger Insurance agency. Then he sold cars for various dealerships. He retired in 1986 from Midwest Ford in Brunswick.

In 1956, he and some friends started the Valley News, a Liverpool Township newspaper. Mr. Naftzger later wrote a column called "Duane's World" for the Medina Town Square Post.

In addition to his wife of 56 years, he is survived by sons, David of Homer Township, Dennis of Liverpool Township and Douglas of Loveland, Colo.; four grandchildren; and two brothers.

Services will be at 11 a.m. tomorrow at Emmanuel United Church of Christ, 6656 Center Rd., Liverpool Township.

Donations may be made to the Hospice of Medina County, 797 N. Court St., Medina 44256.

Bauer Funeral Home of Liverpool Township is handling arrangements.

Chapter 2

Rule No. 1: Make Sure They're Dead

Alana Baranick

In an episode of "The Drew Carey Show," Drew's buddies are reading the newspaper, presumably the Plain Dealer, while waiting for 42-year-old Drew to return to his desk in the Winfred-Louder Department Store office, when his friend Kate discovers an obituary that initially amuses her.

"Some guy named Drew Carey died," Kate tells her comrades. "And he worked for Winfred-Louder." She pauses, as the description of the late Drew Carey sounds too much like her friend. "And he was 42."

They soon learn that Drew's sister-in-law, Mimi, provided the newspaper with a bogus death certificate, which enabled her to get the premature obit printed.

A silly scenario? Sure. But newspapers do demand proof of death before printing an obituary or death notice. Or at least they should. Copies of the death certificate are not usually required. We generally accept the word of funeral directors, cremation society representatives, coroners and other officials. If the body was donated to a medical school for research, we ask authorities in the anatomy department to verify the death.

When an obituary or death notice has run in another newspaper or is reported by a wire service, we trust that our counterparts at the other news agencies have followed the accepted death-test procedure.

Sometimes that doesn't happen. I once worked for a newspaper that printed a premature obit. Luckily it wasn't my fault, but I had to deal with the fallout when a man called to tell me about his mother. She wasn't dead, he said, but she nearly died that morning when she read his obituary in the paper.

Oddly enough, the caller wasn't angry about the obit, but he still wanted to know how this could have happened. Who gave the details of his life and the lie about his death to the reporter who wrote the premature obit?

The answer was simple. A man identifying himself as the brother of the alleged deceased gave the reporter a convincing sob story, complete with biographical details and the name of an out-of-state funeral home where the funeral was to be held. The reporter, working late at night and against deadline, failed to call the funeral home to confirm the death.

If the call to the funeral home had been made, the story would not have seen the light of day. Lesson: Never print the report of a death without confirmation from someone official.

We never learned who perpetrated that hoax. I don't know whether my caller or his mother ever discovered the identity of the culprit. He may have been a friend playing a practical joke or an enemy seeking vengeance. Being a cynic, I also considered the possibility that the faux-obit subject himself may have had some motive for doing the dirty deed.

I've heard other stories from veteran obit writers about scorned lovers and angry spouses who took a stab at killing off their exes in print.

AFTER TERRORISTS HIJACKED COMMERCIAL AIRLINERS and crashed them into the World Trade Center, the Pentagon and a field in Pennsylvania on Sept. 11, 2001, the proof of death required for stories to run in obituary sections became more nuanced.

Those missing in the attacks were like the inhabitants of the planet Alderaan in George Lucas' original "Star Wars" movie. With Princess Leia, we watched Alderaan being blown to bits by the Death Star. And like Obi-Wan Kenobi, we felt "a disturbance in the Force," as "thousands of voices screamed out and suddenly were silenced."

We may never be able to view the bodies of all the victims in the WTC collapse, but we have good reason to believe they died in the horrendous happenings.

Families were holding memorial services before their missing loved ones' remains were found and identified. Official lists of the missing provided us the go-ahead to write about those who were presumed dead in the attacks, but we avoided using the verb "died" unless the bodies had been identified. Instead of death certificates, declarations of death were being issued, but not always as quickly as memorial services were being arranged.

Rule No. 1: Make Sure They're Dead

When we could not use the words "died" or "was declared dead" for the memorial service announcement, we explained where the person was supposed to have been — i.e., on the 104th floor of the north tower — when the World Trade Center collapsed.

A couple of months after the attacks, I asked one woman whether her husband, who was in the uppermost floors of Tower No. 1 when it was hit, had been found, had been declared dead, or was presumed dead. They were, after all, holding a memorial service for him. Somewhat annoyed at me, she answered, "He's not dead. He's missing."

Even though our memorial-service story for one former Clevelander missing in the WTC collapse did not include the word "died," the headline did. I should have warned the headline writer to be careful about this.

In the obituaries I write, I usually mention what funeral home or other agency verified the death. Naming the funeral home gives the readers a way of contacting the family to offer condolences. For me, it's also a matter of attribution, in a sense telling readers, "I didn't put a mirror under this guy's nostrils to make sure he was breathless. I am relying on the word of that person over there."

If the funeral director, cremation society representative or body donation spokesperson is not available, I'll try to get confirmation of the death from the medical examiner or a nursing supervisor at the hospital or nursing home where the person died.

But getting verification of a death from a hospital or nursing home is not always easy, especially since privacy regulations have been stiffened. Some hospital personnel are reluctant to verify a death. They may fear exceeding their authority, or they may distrust my motives. After all, they don't know me. A few times I've had to ask the kin of the deceased to get a medical facility to release the information to me.

I ONCE ASKED A FRENCH-SPEAKING COLLEAGUE to call a funeral home in Quebec to verify the death of a Clevelander who died while on vacation in that Canadian province. She requested the cause of death. I was grateful and impressed. It's hard enough to ask for a cause of death in English.

In the opening scene of "Perfect," John Travolta as fledgling reporter Adam Lawrence is shown doing a telephone interview for an obituary.

"What funeral home was she taken to? How old was she? What did she die of?"

I could almost hear the person on the other end of the phone complaining, "That's none of your business."

Lawrence, the obit writer, says, "I have to know what she died of, or I can't write the obit. I don't make the rules."

Obit writers don't ask for the cause of death because they want to intrude on a family's privacy. They are trying to provide a service to their readers and pacify their editors.

Tell your friends that someone has died, and generally the first thing they'll ask is "What happened?" Especially when the deceased is what would be considered too young to die. Think about it — how could you do an obit for a child and not give the cause of death?

I've interviewed many bereaved relatives who became upset when I asked for the cause of death. They believed that "long illness" or "suddenly" was sufficient. But "died suddenly" creates questions. I know that most often "suddenly" is code for "heart attack" or "stroke," but it could also stand for "self-inflicted gunshot wound" or "head-on collision." Even if we have a chronic illness, death itself happens in an instant — suddenly.

If we say someone died after a "long illness," we want to know what that "long illness" was. If a person was diabetic, went through kidney dialysis and ultimately suffered a heart attack while on the operating table, it would be better to say "died of complications from diabetes" or "had a heart attack," than to leave readers wondering.

Some bereaved relatives won't reveal the cause of death because they worry about what others might think. They prefer to be vague, because they see "AIDS" as a code word for "gay," or "liver disease" as a condition that suggests alcoholism. Others don't want to say "cancer," because they believe drug addicts will break into their homes to steal leftover morphine or other drugs while the family is attending the funeral.

Sometimes the bereaved relatives so intensely despise the illness that claimed their loved one that they just don't want to see the disease's name connected with the dearly departed in the obit. I've seen the same attitude prevail when families don't want us to print the name of the deceased's nasty employer because of their abiding hatred.

Consider the consequences of not explaining why a person who was pre-retirement age died. If we don't offer an explanation or we say, "The family would not disclose the cause of death," the reader may assume that Cousin Barney committed suicide or Uncle Edgar had a heart attack while getting his money's worth from a prostitute.

Did the person die as the result of a traffic accident? A house fire? Carbon monoxide poisoning? A contagious disease that could affect others in the community? A gunshot wound? If so, the newspaper may want to address the death as a news story, rather than as an obituary.

I'll never forget the funeral director who asked whether we could say that his elderly subject had died "after a long illness." The dead fellow did have terminal cancer, but he actually died of a self-inflicted gunshot. He put himself out of his misery.

Rule No. 1: Make Sure They're Dead

Another mortician, when pressed for an answer, told me that the 30-ish woman whose funeral he was arranging had died of complications of childbirth. When I dug for more information, including whether her child survived, I learned that the mortician was simply telling me what her family had told him. He didn't have the death certificate yet. He was waiting for the coroner to rule. The coroner told me that the woman had died of a heart attack — brought on by her heroin addiction. She wasn't pregnant. I had a hard time trusting anything that funeral director told me after that, not because he was dishonest, but because he didn't say, "I don't know."

DAY OF DEATH IS USUALLY NOT A PROBLEM, except for cases in which the person died alone and the body was found days later. Even then, the medical examiner usually can estimate the time of death or at least give a statement, often based on when the person was last seen.

I once received obituary information about a man who was declared brain dead a full day before he actually died. His widow said he died Tuesday. The funeral-home assistant reported the man died Wednesday. We went with Wednesday, which appeared on the death certificate.

Be clear about the location of death. Aunt Fran died in California. That's a pretty big state. Whereabouts in California? Aunt Fran died in San Diego. On the street? At home? In a hospital or nursing home? Aunt Fran died at the Good Samaritan Nursing Home in San Diego. That's better. Even if the newspaper doesn't print the exact location, at least the reporter will know that Aunt Fran didn't get mauled by a lion at the San Diego Zoo.

Many people, particularly older folks, are ashamed to say that their loved one died in a nursing home. They're afraid others will think that they didn't really care about the dearly departed. If they did, they would have given up their jobs to stay at home and personally care for their mother, so she could die at home, surrounded by her loving family.

I say to them, don't feel guilty. Be realistic. Some of us simply are not equipped to be full-time health-care providers.

Did Dad die of a heart attack at home? Or did he have the heart attack at home and die on the way to the hospital? Perhaps he died in the ambulance, but was pronounced dead at the hospital. Maybe he keeled over on a city street or behind the wheel of a car.

Sometimes the circumstances surrounding a death speak volumes about the individual. Readers see the dedication of an elderly musician who suffered a fatal heart attack while driving to his weekly unpaid gig at a nursing home to entertain patients. They are moved by the story of a young mountain climber who died after falling down the cellar steps a couple of days before she was to hike on Mount Ranier.

I once wrote about a man who raised beagles and entered them in field trials. Friends said that it was not the competition that thrilled him. He just enjoyed being outdoors and running his dogs. When the man became ill during a contest about 100 miles from his home, his fellow dog-lovers wanted to take him to a nearby hospital, but he refused. He suffered a heart attack on the way home.

"He died on a mattress in the back of a pickup truck with his dogs," his daughter said. "That's the way he would have liked it."

MADONNA KOLBENSCHLAG, NUN, AUTHOR OF SIX BOOKS

By Alana Baranick, Plain Dealer Reporter

Morgantown, W.Va. — Sister Madonna Kolbenschlag, a Humility of Mary nun and internationally known feminist author who was committed to educating and empowering women, died Friday at a hospital in Santiago, Chile, a day after suffering a stroke. She was 64.

The Cleveland native had been in Chile as a speaker for the School of Ecofeminist Spirituality and Ethics, a two-week international women's conference. Thursday afternoon at the closing ritual of the event, Sister Kolbenschlag told participants that the years she had dedicated to working for and with women were sacred to her.

The first of Sister Kolbenschlag's six books, "Kiss Sleeping Beauty Goodbye," which was published in 1979 and has been translated into five languages, was pivotal in the feminist movement, according to Sister Nancy Sylvester, an Immaculate Heart of Mary nun and national president of the Leadership Conference for Women Religious.

"It was one of the first books for women coming into an understanding of themselves," Sylvester said. "It really touched a whole variety of women who said, 'This makes sense. It's something we need to pay attention to.' It was a pivotal book for its time, and it continues today."

Among her other books are "Eastward Toward Eve" and "Lost in the Land of Oz."

Sister Kolbenschlag, who received a bachelor's degree from Notre Dame College in South Euclid in 1962, broke ground for women in other ways as well. The Women's International Electronic University, which she founded in 1996 to educate and empower women throughout the world via the Internet, is the culmination of her life's work, according to colleagues.

"Madonna was a visionary," Sylvester said. "She committed herself to help low-income women everywhere, women who suffered from abuse and Third World women. For me, she was an inspiration. She kept pushing the boundaries to be creative in how we can use the gospel and serve today's world with today's needs."

Sister Kolbenschlag entered the Humility of Mary order from St. Patrick Catholic Church on Bridge Ave. in Cleveland in 1954. She professed her first vows in 1956 and her final vows in 1959.

She earned a master's degree in English in 1968 and a doctorate in literature in 1973 from the University of Notre Dame in South Bend, Ind. She later earned a master's degree and a doctorate, both in clinical psychology, from the Fielding Institute in Santa Barbara, Calif.

In the late 1950s, Sister Kolbenschlag taught at Villa Maria High School in Pennsylvania. In the 1960s, she was a teacher at Magnificat High School in Rocky River, at St. John High School in Ashtabula and at her high school alma mater, Lourdes Academy in Cleveland.

Sister Kolbenschlag was a professor of American and women's studies at the University of Notre Dame in the 1970s. She was a lecturer at Loyola University in Chicago from 1980 to 1981.

She spent most of the 1980s in Washington, D.C. She was a legislative aide and research consultant in the House of Representatives for six years and was involved in human rights investigations in Central America. She also was a senior fellow of the Woodstock Theological Center at Georgetown University and an ecumenical fellow at the National Cathedral.

Since 1989, she had lived in the Morgantown, W.Va., area. Sister Kolbenschlag was an associate professor of behavioral medicine and psychiatry at the University of West Virginia and a clinical psychologist and research associate with the university's health services. She served three terms as a women's commissioner for the state of West Virginia.

Survivors include her mother, Maude of Fairview Park; and brothers, Joseph of Strongsville and Michael of San Clemente,

Calif.

Services will be at 3 p.m. Friday at Villa Maria Chapel, Villa Maria, Pa. Sister Kolbenschlag's family will receive friends from 7 to 9 p.m. today at McGorray Bros. Funeral Home, 14133 Detroit Ave., Lakewood.

Donations may be made to the Sisters of the Humility of Mary, Villa Maria, Pa., 16155.

Chapter 3

They Call Me Mr. Tibbs

Alana Baranick

In my favorite episode of HBO's "Oz," actor Harold Perrineau, the narrator, bemoans an obituary in which the deceased's name is misspelled.

"It's not like they're gonna get his name right the next time he dies," Perrineau says. "No, that edition of the newspaper is going in the archives. And this guy I know, his name, which is the thing he's probably proudest of in life, it's gonna be wrong. Forever and ever."

Accuracy is imperative in obituary writing. Even when someone who is supposed to know correct spellings has submitted legible information to the newspaper, the reporter must spell back the names of the deceased and the surviving relatives to the funeral director or the family. If there are any discrepancies, get it right before getting it in print.

Filling in the blank under the heading "Name of the deceased" isn't always as easy as it seems. Besides the person's legal name, there are nicknames, professional names, maiden names, married names and previous married names.

Perhaps the most unusual altered moniker I've encountered was that of Edris Eckhardt, an internationally known sculptor, ceramist and enamelist, who invented new processes with which to express her art.

The artist also expressed herself by changing her name. She was born Edythe Aline Eckhardt, but changed her name during her final year of sculpting studies at the Cleveland School of Art in 1931. She had been passed over for a prestigious fellowship in favor of a male student. Presumably, members of the awards committee believed the scholarship would be wasted on a woman, who would most likely marry and raise a family.

That's when Eckhardt gave up her given name for "Edris," which she said was the name of a genderless angel. She also insisted on being called a sculptor rather than a sculptress, a bold act in those days.

Some immigrants and their offspring assume Americanized names or legally change their names. Many go by their foreign monikers inside their ethnic enclaves and by their adjusted names everywhere else. Sometimes the new surname spellings differ from one member of the family to another. This is especially true for names that were not intended to be written with the letters of the Roman alphabet.

The late sportswriter Ed Chay was born with the surname Chylinski. He spelled it "Chilinski" when he joined the military, and legally changed it to "Chay" when he returned to civilian life.

Some folks take on the surname of their adoptive parents. Catholic nuns and Muslim converts may change their names for religious reasons. Entertainers, writers and businessmen may change theirs to fit a marquee or to make it easier to remember.

Transvestites and folks undergoing sex changes present their own unique nom issues. He who was Glen yesterday may be known as Glenda today.

I cited potential gender-bending complications to help support my case for dropping the use of courtesy titles — Mr., Mrs., Miss, Ms. — in obits at the Plain Dealer a few years ago. I disliked having to explain to bereaved relatives why we used "Mr." or "Ms." instead of "Dr." on second reference for folks who held doctorates in philosophy and not in medicine. I agonized over what title was proper for clerics of various religions. I hated deciding what title was appropriate for a much-married, much-divorced woman who went back to using her maiden name. I much prefer not having to think about courtesy titles.

Many newspapers continue to use courtesy titles on second reference in obits, even though these terms are used in other stories only to distinguish same-surnamed characters. As a reporter, you have to go with your paper's policy. But don't be afraid to tell your superiors when you think things ought to be changed.

I like to spell out what name a person was known by at various points in his or her life to help readers identify the body.

This is particularly helpful in identifying women, especially teachers, who had careers before getting married. If your first grade teacher was a single woman when she taught you your ABCs, but was a married woman by the time your cousin was in her class, each of you would remember her by a different moniker.

Before the 1960s, most married women didn't have first names, at least not as far as newspapers were concerned. A woman lost her identity when she took on her husband's surname. Once rings were exchanged, she became Mrs. Insert-Husband's-Name-Here. It becomes more confusing in the case of multiple marriages.

Some folks still aren't enlightened. In recent years I dealt with a funeral director who, like the Taliban in Afghanistan, subscribed to the old ways regarding men, women and their place in society. When giving me obituary information for a child who died of a congenital illness, the funeral director said, "She is survived by her parents, the Rev. and Mrs. John Smith."

"What's the child's mother's name?" I asked.

"Mrs.," he said.

He refused to waver from his stance, as if he would be giving in to what Rush Limbaugh would call a "femi-nazi." For the record, I'm nowhere near being a femi-nazi, and I firmly believe that even Limbaugh would not have agreed with this guy's actions. The woman who gave birth to that child should have her own name in her child's obit. I worked around the misguided funeral director by calling the Rev.'s church to get the mom's name.

Autoworker Peg Crawford's parents couldn't agree on what to name her when she was born. For the first six years of her life, her birth certificate showed her as "Baby Lowery." Her father called her Peggy, while other relatives dubbed her Maureen, Lydia and Patty.

Her mother enrolled her in school as Vivian Maureen Lowery, which became her official name. Yet because her father carried the most weight in the family, she always introduced herself as Peg. For most of her life, she was Peg Crawford, wife of Hansel Crawford.

To OFFSET THE DISMAL ASPECT OF WRITING ABOUT THE DEAD, I tend to take an offbeat view of the names of my subjects and their relatives. I hope, for example, that Pearl White was a dental hygienist. I wonder whether Clay Potter was an artist. Was Bill Coyne a banker or accountant? Did Iona Greathouse really have a fabulous home?

I love the episode of the television sitcom "Taxi" in which Elaine, a cab driver, has to quickly come up with a name for the perfect boyfriend she had invented to impress an old rival. Under pressure from her snooty nemesis, who was seated in the back of her taxi, Elaine looked for inspiration from the urban terrain of New York City. Seeing a billboard ad, she blurted out the first thing that came to mind. "Billboard." Yes. That would be her imaginary boyfriend's name. "Bill Board."

Later, on a double date with fellow cabbie Alex filling in as the boyfriend, Elaine's rival's fiance asks the faux Mr. Board whether he took a lot of ribbing because of his unusual moniker. Alex, alias Bill, responds, "Not as much as my brothers, Clip and Switch."

Even some of my colleagues who don't write obits like to play the name game. Between us we've found some nifty names of the living and the dead that make us smile. Olive Green, Hazel Nutt, Candy Korn, Claude Hopper. I once read a death notice for a man whose first name was Little; his surname, Promise. Little Promise. What were his parents thinking? I hope he exceeded their expectations.

You can imagine how ecstatic I was when, during my daily routine of skimming the fill-in-the-blanks obituary forms faxed to our newsroom, I read about a man whose moniker satisfied my appellation fixation: Happy Laffin.

John O. "Happy" Laffin had a sense of humor that matched his cheerful name. He owned a gas station, which he dubbed "Laffin Gas," and set up his checking accounts so he could sign his checks with Happy Laffin's signature.

His wife shared his chipper attitude. Her name may have been Ida May or Irene Marie. I really couldn't say. She refused to share her full name with strangers. She preferred to use her initials, so that anyone who spoke her name would have to say, "I. M. Laffin."

AN OBITUARY'S PRIMARY PURPOSE is to identify the deceased to a wide audience of readers through biographical information. A person's name can differentiate him from or confuse him with another person.

In the movie "The Terminator," Arnold Schwarzenegger portrays the title character, a futuristic robot-cyborg-whatever that travels into the past to kill a woman named Sarah Connor before she can give birth to the man who years later would lead a rebel band bent on destroying the machines that take over the post-apocalyptic world.

Armed only with Sarah's name, his own inhuman super powers and a computer program with no "end task" command, the Terminator goes about slaughtering every Sarah Connor listed in the telephone book.

The obituary writer at Sarah's local newspaper would have had a field day or a heart attack explaining to the world which Sarah Connor had died.

Readers would want to know whether the late Sarah Connor was Sarah Connor, the 30-year-old cashier who rang up their smoked kielbasa and instant lottery tickets at the supermarket. Or Sarah Connor, the 70-year-old retired geometry teacher who kept them after school to beat chalk dust out of erasers. Or Sarah Connor, the prim and proper pigtailed 10-year-old granddaughter of their next-door neighbor who reminded them of Patty McCormack in "The Bad Seed."

I have never written about any Sarah Connors, but I have penned obits for many other same-named individuals. While you might expect that I would write about a lot of John Smiths, Robert Joneses and Mary Millers, and I have encountered many of them, other names may be more common in a given area, depending on the population's ethnicity, religion and roots.

I've heard about an Amish town where half the men are named John Stultzfus. In Greater Cleveland, we have many Helen Toths from the Hungarian neighborhoods, Jose Rodriguezes in the Hispanic community, John Corrigans of Irish descent, and Willie Browns, male and female, among African Americans. Many names cross gender, ethnic, racial and religious boundaries.

Sometimes names aren't identical, but they're similar enough to be confusing, especially if their death notices are printed in the same paper. When Margaret E. Wood, a homemaker and candy maker whose family called her "Aunt Marg," and Marguerette Wood, a formidable softball pitcher who was better known as "Marge," died a day apart, I wrote obits for both of them. Their respective stories were printed on the same page.

We ran a photo of Cleveland financial planner Michael J. Fox with his obituary, so readers would know instantly that this was not the beloved television and film star of the same name. The Cleveland Fox, who died of cancer, had grown accustomed to the confusion that went with having the same name as the celebrity Fox, whose Parkinson's disease diagnosis made headlines across the country.

When actor Fox's "Family Ties" TV series was popular, teenage girls who found the Cleveland Fox's name in the phone book would call his home either as a prank or out of a sincere hope of talking with their Hollywood heartthrob.

The lesser known Fox bought a house in 1986 while the famous actor was in Cleveland making the movie, "Light of Day." A clerk, seeing the name on the real estate transaction, started rumors that the West Coast movie star was moving to the North Coast.

In a quickie Internet search, I found more than 60 Michael J. Foxes with listed telephone numbers in the United States and more than 100 Janet Jacksons, Edward Kennedys and George Bushes.

GEORGE CAREY BUSH, LTV STEEL MANAGER

BY ALANA BARANICK, PLAIN DEALER REPORTER
Bay Village — George Carey Bush, a retired LTV Steel Co.

executive whose presidential-sounding name brought him national attention, died of a heart attack Wednesday at his home in Bay Village.

Bush, 76, was eight months younger than former President George Herbert Walker Bush and bore a slight resemblance to him. That was enough to confuse reporters when he visited Washington, D.C., on business in August 1974.

At that time Gerald Ford, who became president after the resignation of Richard Nixon, was deciding whether to nominate Nelson Rockefeller or the lesser-known George H.W. Bush as his vice president.

George C. Bush was paged by friends after arriving at Dulles Airport on the day that Ford announced Rockefeller's nomination. Reporters at the airport, who heard, "Message for George Bush," on the public address system, swarmed around the clueless traveler, thinking he was the loser of the vice presidential sweepstakes.

Bush, a Bay Village resident for the last 16 years, enjoyed the sporadic ribbing he took as the other Bush rose to national prominence. Yet he never anticipated the commotion that would result from his ordering a pizza around the time that his namesake became the 41st president of the United States.

A suburban newspaper interviewed him after receiving a tip from the pizza shop. Other newspapers followed. He also was featured on morning talk radio programs across the country. Paul Harvey shared a snippet of his story with his national radio audience. Bush's media fling peaked when he appeared on television with Johnny Carson on "The Tonight Show."

Bush was known as Carey while growing up in his native Pittsburgh. He became more widely known as George while serving with the 15th Air Force during World War II. He provided ground support for the 483rd Bomb Group's 840th Bomb Squadron in Europe as a radar specialist, while the future American president was a Navy pilot, flying missions in the Pacific.

During his 45-year career as a traffic manager, overseeing shipping for steel mills, Bush spoke several times before the Interstate Commerce Commission, Congress and the Department of Transportation about industrial traffic issues.

He was vice president of the Pittsburgh Traffic Club when the other Bush was vice president [of the United States]. He chaired the American Iron and Steel Institute transportation committee and also headed National Industrial Traffic League panels.

Bush moved to Cleveland with Jones & Laughlin Steel Co., which merged with Republic Steel Corp. to become LTV Steel Co. He retired as general manager of traffic for LTV in 1993.

Survivors include his wife of 52 years, Jeanne; sons, Steven C. of Scarsdale, N.Y., and Timothy A. of New York City; daughter, Karen J. of New York City; two grandchildren; and a brother.

Burial will be private.

Donations may be made to the National World War II Memorial, American Battle Monuments Commission, P.O. Box 96766, Washington, D.C. 20090-6766.

Arrangements are by Berry Funeral Home of Westlake.

Chapter 4

Age Ain't Nothin' But a Number

Alana Baranick

My sister doesn't want anyone to know her age, even when she's dead.

I believe it's a notion that took hold of her when she was in her 20s or 30s and could still pass for a teenager. It's not like people can't do the math when they meet her sons or hear about her grandchildren. I keep telling her that if I looked as good as she does, I'd be bragging about my age. Why cover it up?

Yet her obsession is shared by others. I frequently get requests from bereaved relatives to omit their loved one's age from the obit. "She never wanted anyone to know," they often say. Or, "I promised her I'd never reveal her age. She'll come back from the grave to haunt me."

Some folks won't break their oath of secrecy even when I explain that our paper probably won't print the story without including the age. Even though I can usually find the date of birth through public-record databases, I won't write the obit unless the family will confirm the age. Unless, of course, the dearly departed was a public figure — an elected official, movie star or other type of celebrity.

Sometimes when people won't share the age of a sibling or a spouse I wonder whether it might be because they don't want to make a statement about their own ages. I knew a woman whose youthful-looking husband was old enough to be her father. She didn't want his age printed when he died because people might believe that she was in his age bracket. The same reasoning may apply when a woman's younger brother dies.

Age Ain't Nothin' But a Number

If we say he was 79, then we're saying that she must be 80 or older.

West Killings' children didn't know what age to provide for his obituary, which was printed in the Plain Dealer on March 6, 1993. They were sure the former highway worker was older than the age noted in official records. Instead of saying that Killings was this old or that age, his obituary explained why we couldn't be sure.

> His exact age was unknown. He was born in Laurel, Miss., before the census was taken in 1910.
>
> "At that time, they said he was 4 years old," his daughter recalled. "But he said he was older than that. He remembered that he was taken out of school to work in the fields" the day the census was taken.
>
> Because his family did not have a birth certificate for him, the Census Bureau recorded his birth date as April 15, 1906. But he told his daughter that he was born in March.

Lena Roberson was born to former slaves in Birdsville, Ky., on April 15, 1894, and died a week after her 106th birthday. She used a copy of a 1900 census form — listing her parents and their 6-year-old daughter — as her birth certificate. The Social Security Administration accepted the census form as proof of her age when determining retirement benefits.

Her cousin, who was in her 80s when Roberson died, didn't know Roberson's exact age, but agreed that she had to be around 106. The cousin remembered that when she was a small child, Roberson was already an adult.

Age can also tell you whether it's reasonable to say that a person was a pioneer in his field or founded a company. If a man was 62 years old when he died, chances are he was not the founder of his family-owned business that was started 55 years ago. If Daddy was born in the early 1950s, when comedian Milton Berle reigned as Mr. Television, then Daddy was not a pioneer in television repair.

When the deceased seems rather young to have been considered a leading authority in his field, I conduct additional research and interviews to make sure it's true. Don't dismiss such claims. Some folks achieve success before their hair turns gray.

Until the 1980s it was a newsmaking event when a person reached his 100th birthday. Nowadays people are living longer, and centenarians are more commonplace. As a result we write fewer obituaries for people simply because they passed the century mark. We're more interested in knowing what they did during more than a century of living and whether their activities, lifestyle and/or attitude contributed to their longevity.

KNOWING A PERSON'S AGE CAN HELP an obituary writer determine whether other biographical information provided by the family or the funeral home can be believed.

I once interviewed a man who told me his father served in the Army during World War II. This was impossible. His father, who was born around 1940, might have been old enough for kindergarten by the time the Allies won the war in 1945, but certainly not old enough for military service. The government gave "World War II veteran" status to people who served during the occupation of Japan or Germany after the war was officially over. But no matter how you add it up, this fellow could not have been a WWII vet.

When I told the son that the math didn't work, he asked, "What war came after WWII?" I told him it was the Korean War. He replied, "Well, then it was the Korean War."

No. I don't think so. His dad would have been 13 or 14 when that war ended, still too young to participate.

"But he had to have served in World War II," the young man said with the utmost sincerity. "We've got pictures of him in his Army uniform when he was in Germany."

Poor fellow. In his mind, "Germany" plus "Army" equals "WWII." He couldn't fathom that anyone could serve in the military in Germany (actually, it was West Germany then) during peace time.

You don't have to have a command of history to do obits, but it helps to have enough understanding of the 20th century to question whether what you've been told makes sense. When in doubt about anything, look it up.

A FULL AND MOST WONDERFUL LIFE; 'AGELESS' BROOKLYN WOMAN HELPED OTHER WOMEN FEEL VITALITY

BY ALANA BARANICK, PLAIN DEALER REPORTER

Brooklyn — Statuesque, bright-eyed and vivacious, the sexagenarian grandmother drew admiring glances whether dressed in an elegant gold satin gown or in tight, black leather pants with red high-heeled boots.

Her friends say that Betty Ann Savage, who died of a heart attack Feb. 25, looked 20 years younger than her 66 years. She never talked about age - hers or anyone else's.

"You're fabulous right now," she would tell shoppers trying on mother-of-the-bride outfits at Pen-E-Ventures, the boutique she had managed since 1996. Upon finding the perfect dress for her client, she would moisten her thumb with her tongue, touch her thumb to the woman's backside and make a hissing sound: "Ssss. Sssee? You sssizzle!"

She could make even the frumpiest women believe they were glamorous.

"She put their hair up on top of the head with a clip, and it was like magic," said shop owner Penny Dixon. "It was a lot more than just putting a dress on. She made them feel good about themselves."

Savage's fairy godmother routine didn't stop when she left the shop. If she went to a party and encountered a woman in a blue mood, she would take her upstairs, fix her hair and make-up, add a scarf or piece of jewelry and say, "Now, let's go have fun!"

Before helping start the special-occasion dress shop, Savage did makeovers for housewives and career women at the Estee Lauder cosmetics counter at Higbee's, later Dillard's, in downtown Cleveland.

Business executives looking for gifts for their wives or employees asked for her by name. Street people, like the man who rode the escalator all day, also stopped at Savage's counter for a kind word or a couple of bucks.

"She didn't treat them differently," said former co-worker Marguerite Moran. "That was the secret. She treated them all the same. She was never judgmental. You could tell her anything."

Savage, whose maiden name was Chuha, was 8 when her father died. She and her older sister, Dorothy, were raised by their widowed mother in Cleveland in the 1940s.

Young Betty spent summers in the country at a camp for underprivileged city kids and at an uncle's farm on Brecksville Road at Ohio 21. Years later, she would learn that during that period her future husband, Don Savage, lived across the street from the farm. They didn't meet until both were sophomores at South High School.

Before marrying Don in April 1955, Betty modeled bridal gowns and greeted customers at Higbee's Silver Grill. She worked as a roller-skating carhop before becoming a stay-at-home mom, a role she relished.

Savage didn't let her mild heart condition slow her down.

When her children - Denise LaRosa, now of Marietta, Ga., and Michael and Jeffrey, both of Medina - were young, she played baseball or shot baskets with them and other youngsters in her Brooklyn neighborhood. As she got older, she liked to swim and ice skate with her grandchildren.

She kept a basket filled with fruit and another with vitamin bottles on her kitchen counter. She cooked with herbs, tomatoes and zucchini from her garden. She also cultivated several flower beds.

"She'd pinch off tops of flowers so they'd grow and get new buds," her daughter said. "It must have worked. Her gardens were spectacular. She accessorized them with hanging baskets and butterflies and angels."

In recent years, Betty and Don went on cruises with four other couples.

"She found wonderment in the most insignificant little things," said cruise-mate Moran. "We'd be walking along. She'd see a little lizard or a little flower, and she'd say, 'Oh, my God! What's this?' "

The group was planning a cross-country road trip for next year. Betty, who had visited the Dominican Republic, Belize, Hawaii and, last summer, Alaska, was looking forward to finally seeing the Grand Canyon.

"We had nothing but good experiences," her husband said. "We saw the rain forest, glaciers, pyramids in Mexico, whales.

"She loved every minute of it."

Chapter 5

Dig a Little Deeper

ALANA BARANICK

A lot of the obit job is formula writing, but it can be fun. Yes, "fun," as in "We put the 'fun' in funerals."

Approach the task of penning post-mortems as a challenge. Be a detective. Contact a few of the deceased's friends, colleagues and relatives for a different perspective. Dig in the library for information to support, enhance or refute what you have already been told.

I will never forget writing the obituary of George Ostro Jr., a 48-year-old man who was alone at home when he suffered a fatal heart attack. He was dead for three days before a neighbor became worried enough to call sheriff's deputies.

His funeral arrangements were being handled by one of my favorite morticians — a man who personally knew many of his clients and relished relating colorful stories about them. But all he could tell me about Ostro was that he was a loner who had worked at a second-hand store owned by his late mother in a rural town with a population of 200.

I told the funeral director that perhaps I would find for more information about Ostro in the morgue. No, not the place where the coroner puts bodies on ice. "Morgue" is journalist-speak for the newspaper's archives or library. The funeral director assured me, "You won't find anything on old George."

Lo and behold! I found an envelope with Ostro's name on it in the morgue. To my surprise, I learned that he had taken out petitions from the board of elections! To run for president! Of the United States! Three times!

Ostro never collected enough signatures to get his name on the ballot, but he got his message out through interviews with local reporters during the presidential election campaigns of 1972, 1976 and 1980. He ran as an independent, a fitting classification for a man who would have cut taxes by 75 to 99 percent, abolished Congress and revised the Constitution.

I've found a lot of information on freshly dead subjects in old newspaper clippings. Retirement stories and profiles are especially helpful in establishing a timeline and getting an overall picture of the person's life.

Sometimes you can find unexpected information in a special-event announcement, the coverage of a public meeting or a list of award winners. I love uncovering little gems that accentuate some fascinating aspect of the deceased's life that his family or friends didn't know or had forgotten.

Finding the dearly departed's words in print can be enlightening and poignant. Leslie E. Jones was interviewed a year before her death for a story about a fund-raising race for breast cancer research. I used information from that article in her obituary, which ran Sept. 6, 1999.

> Last September, Leslie E. Jones, wearing a pink cap identifying her as a breast cancer survivor, managed to walk the one-mile course of the Komen Northeast Ohio Race for the Cure, which raises money for breast cancer research.
>
> "I'm fighting for my life, I know that," Mrs. Jones, weakened by a then six-year bout with the disease, told an interviewer. "Unless a miracle comes along, the prognosis is poor. But seeing all the pink caps, each one a survivor, is like walking with hope. ... I'm hoping that next year I can be here, too."
>
> Mrs. Jones, a spokeswoman for the national Susan G. Komen Breast Cancer Foundation, founder of its Northeast Ohio affiliate and member of the executive committee of its Cleveland fund-raising race, died of complications from the disease Friday at her home in South Russell. She was 51.

It still gives me chills.

BE AWARE THAT YOU CAN'T ALWAYS BELIEVE EVERYTHING you read. The reporter who wrote the original story may have made some factual errors. Or the stories might be filled with unsubstantiated stories told to the reporter by the now-deceased. The same could be said about any other reference materials and, of course, the Internet. It's just the reality of research.

Computer databases are only as reliable as the information that is typed into them. If a name is misspelled in the database or by the researcher, it may never be found. Terms like "county," "saint" or "building" may be abbreviated, sometimes unconventionally, making it even more difficult in online searches.

If the deceased was prominent, you may find biographical info in various editions of "Who's Who." Bear in mind that the entries in books of this nature are provided by the person listed. Although we might think that you can't get anything better than straight-from-the-horse's-mouth data, you must consider the possibility that the horse may be lying through his teeth.

Biographies and autobiographies are wonderful resources, but tend to be impractical when you're working on deadline. They are invaluable if you're working on an advance obit for someone famous.

Old city directories are helpful. These are not telephone directories, but huge books that list local residents, their housemates, their addresses and their occupations. Nowadays, we have criss-cross directories that tell us who lives at what address and, in many cases, their phone numbers, but they don't often include occupations and such.

Thanks to a variety of research tools, including those used by genealogists, I've been able to piece together a person's past with minimal information. One such person was Earl Rutland, a man with cerebral palsy who lived in institutions for 65 years before he died at age 83.

A few weeks before his 18th birthday in 1938, the Cleveland native was committed to an institution for the mentally retarded. By the 1960s he was living at a nursing home, where he did odd jobs and ran errands to earn his keep. For the last 40 years of Rutland's life, no relatives visited him. Folks at the nursing home thought he was orphaned at a young age and had no other family.

Armed with nothing but Rutland's birth certificate, I set out trying to reconstruct his past. City directories and county online marriage records showed that by the time Rutland was 7 years old, his father and mother were no longer married, and his father had a second wife.

What happened to Rutland's mom? I checked the Cleveland Public Library's online necrology files, thinking perhaps his mother had died in childbirth. I didn't find death records for either of his parents, but I did find them for other members of his family. Some of them included Rutland's mother among the surviving relatives.

Clues in the death notices led me to the family's preferred funeral home, located in a rural county 70 miles from Cleveland. The retired funeral director pointed me toward the area's unofficial historian, who had access to death records, school yearbooks and street directories that offered morsels of data about Rutland and his family.

The historian also gave me the phone number of a woman from Rutland's old neighborhood, who turned out to have been a childhood friend. She had fond and vivid recollections of the kind, helpful boy whose peculiar posture and movements struck fear in some folks in the tiny hamlet. She said she'd often wondered, "What ever happened to Earl?"

Here's what happened to him in a nutshell. He was raised by his maternal grandmother and lived not far from his mother, who had remarried. His father dropped out of his son's life. His mother gave birth to a daughter three years before Rutland was placed in an institution. Rutland outlived all of those relatives. His late half sister's children knew they had an Uncle Earl, but believed he was long dead.

It was not unusual in the 1930s for kids like Rutland to be sent away, discarded by family and erased from community memory.

LOTS OF THINGS CHANGE OVER THE COURSE OF HISTORY. What holds true today may not have been the case in days gone by.

Don't equate past stardom in the sports arena with wealth. Professional athletes may become filthy rich through multimillion-dollar contracts and endorsement deals nowadays. But decades ago, sports superstars had to find other work in the off-season to support their families and pay for modest homes in working-class neighborhoods. Most athletes pursued their sport of choice for the love of the game more than for the big bucks.

Obits give us a chance to show how different life was just a few decades ago, especially for women, blacks and blue-collar workers. Collective bargaining was not always available to American workers. And once labor unions became more common, membership was not necessarily open to everyone due to racism, sexism or other factors.

Better-paying factory jobs often were reserved for men. Women who could perform the same duties were paid less. A lot of that changed as the result of the Civil Rights Act enacted by Congress in 1964 and its subsequent amendments.

Legislation may be on the books, but it isn't etched in stone. Even laws can be changed.

For much of the first half of the 20th century, only single women were permitted to teach in many public school districts. It had something to do with the notion that if a woman had snagged a husband to support her, she didn't need to work outside the home. According to the "barefoot and pregnant" creed, she should help the economy by letting a married man with a family or a single woman with no immediate marital prospects have her job, while she, the married woman, concentrated on housekeeping and childrearing.

I once wrote an obit for a newly wed teacher who felt she should be able to continue in her chosen profession until she was ready to stay home. She and several other teachers undergoing similar experiences filed a lawsuit to overturn the school board policy. They won the precedent-setting case and were reinstated.

When searching archives for biographical information on women before the 1960s, be aware that news stories about them might be filed under their husbands' names, possibly with a "Mrs." in front of it. I've found news clippings about several elderly society women combined with those of their late husbands' in our dead files.

The names of countries, corporations, colleges and church denominations, crucial to an obit, may change over time. Was the deceased born in Slovakia, Czechoslovakia or the Czech Republic? Did he retire from Standard Oil of Ohio, Sohio or BP Oil Co.? Was his alma mater Case Institute of Technology, Western Reserve University or the merger of the two institutions, Case Western Reserve University?

Compare the dates in question with what you find in the encyclopedia or in the archives.

When in doubt, I find the safest way to avoid mistakes is to use the phrase "what is now known as." "She graduated from what is now Case Western Reserve University." Or find some other way to sidestep specifics. If you can't nail down exact dates or the name of a man's employer at his retirement, you might be able to say: "He began his career at Standard Oil of Ohio in the 1950s and stayed with the company for more than 40 years."

LIBRARIES, BOTH PUBLIC AND THOSE AVAILABLE ONLY to newspaper personnel, have books on their shelves with more accumulated data than we can fathom. I can go to our paper's research room and find books that show the candidates and vote counts in statewide elections going back to 1966; products made by every manufacturing plant in Ohio; anyone who ever had an at-bat in Major League Baseball; and the histories of Cleveland and neighboring communities.

The Internet also is a treasure trove of information. Biographies of executives, histories of businesses, and officers of professional and service organizations often can be found on the World Wide Web.

Our newspaper has its own electronic library and has access to LexisNexis, an extensive database of print and broadcast media archives. I can search recent stories on other newspapers' online sites through www.newspapers.com or www.onlinenewspapers.com.

I use www.switchboard.com or www.anywho.com to look for phone numbers and addresses. Www.placesnamed.com is a wonderful site for making sure that I'm spelling the names of towns correctly. My favorite search engine at this time is www.google.com. I've googled to find everything from a college professor's resume to the rules for Gaelic football.

I have links to local and state government sites through which I can check criminal records, names of public officials and historical information. I also connect frequently with chambers of commerce and historical societies.

Consult your librarian, computer guru or adolescent son for more Web-searching tips.

LOVE BLOOMED IN WARTIME; INTERNMENT CAMP LED MAN TO FUTURE WIFE, CAREER

By Alana Baranick, Plain Dealer Reporter

Broadview Heights — More than a dozen fishing rods, custom-made by their owner for maximum efficiency and beauty, stand at attention at their assigned post on a wall in the Matsuoka family's split-level home.

Several more poles lean against the fireplace in an adjoining room. A few rest in a white plastic bucket near a rod-wrapping machine, where Jim Matsuoka, retired chairman of Intercole Inc., was fine-tooling them before he died of multiple ailments Dec. 11, at age 82.

Matsuoka's confinement with other Japanese-Americans in relocation camps during World War II fortuitously led to a successful business career that allowed the California native to travel the world and cast lines at his favorite fishing holes.

It also led to the most significant catch of his life: his wife of 60 years, Dassie.

Matsuoka, whose given name was Toshio, and his future wife were students at different universities when American soldiers, in the name of national security, herded them and their families into horse stalls at the Santa Anita Racetrack in 1942, to await relocation to camps in other parts of the country.

"That's where we met," Dassie Matsuoka said. "That was our consolation. It must have been love at first sight. My girlfriend introduced us. She liked him and didn't want to visit him when his sisters were not around, so she took me along" as a chaperone.

The girlfriend may have regretted that decision. Matsuoka was immediately attracted to her pretty companion and used a display of humor to catch her attention.

"He was showing off for me by falling off the chair backwards," his widow said. "He was trying to be funny."

Before long, she was hooked. Within a few months, they were married at the Jerome Relocation Center in Arkansas.

In 1943, the War Relocation Authority found him a job as a machinist at Stewart Bolling & Co. and sent Matsuoka to Cleveland with $50 and a peacoat. His pregnant wife remained at camp until after the birth of the first of their five daughters.

"He was the third Japanese-American in Cleveland," his wife said. "I know it must not have been pleasant."

Because of America's war with Japan, Japanese-Americans often were perceived as the enemy, his family said. Many Stewart Bolling workers gave their new co-worker a cold reception because of his ethnicity, according to his longtime friend Bob Larson. The chill finally wore off after Matsuoka entered management in the 1950s.

"He gained their respect because he expanded the business, and he was fair about advancing people," said Larson, a labor relations lawyer. "Jim was very creative about helping people develop skills that they could use. He became a favorite guy. He just got his sleeves rolled up and did a tremendous job. People saw he was a great leader."

Matsuoka took the first steps from plant floor of the rubber-and-plastics-equipment manufacturer to top administrative offices of its later incarnation, Intercole, by inventing devices that earned him hundreds of U.S. and international patents. He later advanced to sales and administration.

"He was able to see a design in his head, translate that to paper, build it, travel the world and sell it, cost it out, while running the company at home," said his daughter Louise of Las Vegas.

When his daughters — Louise, Arlene Cole, now of Providence, R.I., Nancy Stern and Marie Ashmus, both of Bay Village, and Marilyn Miyamoto of Fairfax, Va. — were young, Matsuoka worked full time Monday through Saturday and half-days on Sundays. His work often took him to Europe, Asia and South America, where he sold equipment, built tire plants and bought clothing and jewelry for the women in his household.

That didn't leave much time for fishing. When he did find the time, Matsuoka took his daughters to a local waterway, where they trolled for fish with handmade poles and lead sinkers. As his professional life became less hectic, he was able to take more and longer fishing excursions with family and friends.

"He loved to catch the big tunas," Larson said. "Whenever he went fishing in California, he'd catch tuna, have it canned and bring canned tuna back to us."

Matsuoka also went on many fishing trips to Cape Cod. He always stayed at the Herring Run Motel in Buzzards Bay, Mass., which, as its name suggests, features a herring run, an excellent source of bait for catching striped bass. He later bought the place to guarantee his access to the herring pond, according to his family.

He loved taking his children and eight grandchildren, whom he taught to fish at an early age, and his sons-in-law on long road trips to destinations where the fish were plentiful.

"My very favorite memories of my grandpa were of him fishing," his granddaughter Emmy Ashmus said at his funeral. "I remember how well he could tie fishing knots and how excited he was when he had a fish on his line."

Chapter 6

What Would Ernie Pyle Do?

ALANA BARANICK

Journalists are supposed to be objective observers, reporting what their five senses take in, not revealing their personal opinions or slanting stories to favor their views.

In my resolve to keep up a neutral front, I do not sign petitions, display political signs in my yard or speak to strangers about my religious beliefs. You won't see an American flag pinned to my jacket lapel or sticking to my car's bumper, even when our country is at war.

Yet I can't hide the stars and stripes that are reflected in the sentimental mist in my eyes when I hear our national anthem belted out before a baseball game or hear about the deaths of veterans who put their lives on the line to preserve our freedoms.

I confess: My quiet patriotism affects my work. I'm partial to writing obituaries about people who served in the Armed Forces. Their stories can be inspiring, while offering some lessons in history, especially when those vets received high honors in times of war.

OBIT WRITERS NEED BASIC TRAINING in military terminology — branches, ranks, decorations and years of major conflicts — along with the dead vet's military records to recreate an accurate depiction of the deceased's life in uniform.

You could request the decedent's military record from the National Personnel Records Center in St. Louis, Mo., but it could take several weeks or forever to get it. The funeral director or the family should be able to share their copies of those papers with you.

The military record should include such items as the veteran's dates of entry and separation, dates of overseas service, unit with which the deceased served, rank attained and decorations earned. These facts may not enable you to pen the kind of powerful tales that legendary war correspondent Ernie Pyle composed from the front lines during World War II. But you can at least verify or discount what the family tells you and piece together a credible outline of the individual's wartime service.

Dad may have been stationed at Pearl Harbor at some time during WWII, but if his date of entry into the military was January 1942, then he was not a survivor of the Japanese attack on the famous Hawaii naval base on Dec. 7, 1941. You can and should check the dates of any campaign, event or project of any war through history books or Web sites.

I had never heard of Operation Blind Bat before I wrote an obit for Timothy Kenski, a Vietnam War veteran who received the Silver Star and the Air Medal for his service with the Air Force. By searching the World Wide Web, I gained an understanding of how this group of airmen flew aircraft in the dark and directed bombing strikes for attack aircraft by dropping flares to mark targets. Combining details from his Silver Star citation, data from Vietnam War chronologies and Web pages of other Blind Bat veterans, I produced an obit that included a simple yet exciting account of Kenski's heroism.

He was a loadmaster on an unarmed C-130 flare airplane, which acted as a forward air controller. On Jan.15, 1968, his aircraft was hit by anti-aircraft fire, which started a blaze among flares in the cargo hold. Ignoring smoke and flames, Kenski entered the flare compartment and jettisoned the load to prevent the C-130 from exploding. He saved the plane and its nine crewmen.

Kenski was 53 when he died of kidney failure in 2000. After the obit I wrote for him was passed around on the Internet, I heard from some of his Air Force buddies who had lost track of him.

SOME TIME-RELATED INFORMATION ON THE MILITARY RECORD can be confusing. The date associated with an award for an individual act of valor could be the day on which the act took place, the date on which the award was issued or the date on which the medal was presented to the war hero.

Soldiers who served in the occupation of Japan or Germany were officially classified as WWII vets, even if they weren't in uniform until 1946.

WWII vets were given many well-deserved considerations that can mess with your mathematical mindset. Many received their high school diplomas while serving overseas. Others earned college degrees quickly in the states through accelerated programs.

What Would Ernie Pyle Do?

Let's say that Uncle Bill joined the Navy in 1943 and got a job at the steel mill immediately after the war. Yet he retired from the steel mill in 1973 with 30 years of service. How can that be? Answer: The steelmaker added the steelworker's years of military service to his time at the mill for retirement benefit purposes.

I try to avoid including specific dates and numbers of years in cases like the aforementioned, when I believe it could confuse the reader. When writing obits, you don't have to include every tidbit of information that comes your way. When in doubt, be vague.

Military ranks of the various branches of the service are listed in the Associated Press Stylebook. If you're going to cite the deceased's rank, it's best to say, "He attained the rank of sergeant," or "He left the military with the rank of sergeant and a Purple Heart."

The structure of the military forces, from squads and platoons to divisions and headquarters commands, is explained in Ed Offley's "Pen & Sword: A Journalist's Guide to Covering the Military" (Marion Street Press, Inc.). This information is especially helpful in defining the group with which the late veteran served.

I don't always include the rank that the veteran attained or the specific division with which he served in the obituary. Nor do I include all the decorations the veteran received. I think in terms of what each award means and which ones set the deceased apart from the rest of the crowd.

WWII Victory Medal signifies that the deceased served in the military during the Second World War. The Korean Service Medal says the same about the dearly departed's service during the Korean War. Other appropriately named medals were given for veterans participating in other military actions. If you've said, "He served in World War II," adding that he received the WWII Victory Medal is redundant.

We hope they all got Good Conduct Medals, just as we hope that all mothers loved their kids unconditionally and that all fathers went out of their way to help their children and grandchildren. It's not something that needs to be listed in an obit.

Some medals, often carrying abbreviations, give an indication of where the person served. ETO equals European Theater of Operations. CIB means China-India-Burma. EAME stands for the European-African-Middle-Eastern theater. "Theater" designations tell you that the veteran served under the command of the general in charge of all military operations of those geographic areas. When possible, specify that your veteran "served in Italy and North Africa" or "participated in the Philippine Liberation."

Most EAME and Asiatic-Pacific theater ribbons carry small bronze battle stars. Each star represents a specific campaign in which the veteran participated. Those campaigns, such as North Africa, Central Europe and Rhineland, usually are listed on the decedent's military record.

Don't confuse bronze battle stars with the prestigious Bronze Star Medal, for which the veteran was singled out for valor or meritorious service. There's usually a story to share about how the person earned the Bronze Star Medal or any other special award. It's unlikely, although not impossible, that someone who served only a few years in the military would receive several Bronze Star Medals.

When trying to evaluate the significance of honors or likelihood that a person who didn't have a long military career received them, I think of Audie Murphy. Murphy, a Texas farm boy, was propelled to national prominence and a Hollywood movie career by virtue of becoming the most decorated soldier of World War II. He held the "most decorated" title until his death in 1971.

But in 1980, another WWII hero, Matt Urban, became tied with Murphy in the most-decorated-of-WWII sweepstakes when he was presented the Medal of Honor by President Jimmy Carter after a long overdue review of his extraordinary war record.

When Urban died in 1995, many newspapers carried obits that recognized that he "may have been" the most decorated soldier of that war. The New York Times settled the issue by getting the numbers from the veterans archives in St. Louis. Both Murphy and Urban received 29 medals during that one war. Career soldiers could collect even more honors during the course of several decades of service.

MURPHY'S SPECIFIC HONORS HELP ME RANK MEDALS by importance. He received the Medal of Honor, the highest award a service person can get. Medal of Honor-ees are so few, you can find out who they are and read their biographies on the Internet at: www.cmohs.org. The Web site bears the name "Congressional Medal of Honor Society," even though that is not the official name of the award. Keep in mind that although the information probably is accurate, the Web site may not be up to date.

Murphy also was awarded the Distinguished Service Cross, which follows the MOH on the top-honors list. (The Air Force equivalent is the Air Force Cross, and the equivalent for marines, sailors and coast guardsmen is the Navy Cross.) You can learn more about military decorations at www.defenselink.mil/specials/ribbons.

His other most impressive awards were the Legion of Merit, Silver Star with Oak Leaf Cluster and Bronze Star with Oak Leaf Cluster. "Oak Leaf Cluster" indicates that he earned more than one of those awards.

He also received five Purple Hearts. That translates to "He was wounded five times." When told that an obit subject was a Purple Heart recipient, I generally ask about the nature of the wound, under what circumstances it happened and whether it left the veteran with any long-lasting impediment, such as a limp, blindness or scar.

I once wrote an obit for a World War I Army private who received the Purple Heart after he was exposed to mustard gas in the trenches in France because his gas mask was faulty. A malignancy later developed in his throat, and his voice box had to be removed.

I always wonder whether Vietnam veterans who died too young of cancer were exposed to Agent Orange. Agent Orange was a defoliant containing the toxic chemical dioxin, which was used to clear away jungle vegetation during the war.

One WWII airman whose obit I wrote broke his leg after parachuting from a plummeting B-24 and landing on a rock pile in enemy territory. Partisans, who made a practice of rescuing Allied airmen, hid the wounded bomber crewman until German soldiers gave up their search. Then they carried him on a stretcher over the mountains to a British field hospital.

It's great to be able to share the story of wartime heroics, but many veterans never talk to their families about what they did in combat, or they play down their own achievements. These are the veterans who routinely say (or said), "The real heroes never came home."

GET YOUR TERMINOLOGY FOR MILITARY folks and branches straight. Soldiers and sailors are not the same animal. Soldiers serve in the Army. Sailors in the Navy. Members of the Marine Corps are called marines. Airmen are just what the name implies: pilots, navigators and other members of aircraft crews.

The evolution of the Air Force is more involved than I can explain here. You can find its detailed history on the Internet at: www.af.mil. (The Army is at www.army.mil; Navy, www.navy.mil; Marine Corps, www.usmc.mil; Coast Guard, www.uscg.mil. You can find other military links through the Department of Defense at www.defenselink.mil.)

Obit writers need to know that the Air Service of the U.S. Army was established in 1918, during World War I. There were earlier air corps incarnations, but it's doubtful you'll be writing about those flyboys.

The flying force went through assorted reorganizations and monikers over the next 30 years, while it was an extension of the Army. It was the Army Air Corps from 1926 until the War Department officially recognized it as the Army Air Forces in 1942. But the Army Air Corps name remained in the common vernacular and on many military records and letterheads throughout WWII.

The Air Force became a separate military branch in 1947.

Don't confuse the Marine Corps with the Merchant Marine (singular), a civilian auxiliary of the Armed Forces. Members of the Merchant Marine definitely played a key role in support of the troops. They put their lives on the line while carrying supplies across the seas in support of the Navy during WWII.

I FIND THAT WIDOWS WHOSE HUSBANDS were the right age but did not serve in the Armed Forces during WWII tend to go on the defensive when I ask, "Did he serve in the military?"

As I understand it, most able-bodied young American men who didn't have families to support enlisted or were drafted for wartime service in the first half of the 1940s. Folks who lived through that era feel they must give a reason if their loved one did not wear his country's uniform.

Many, especially those with special skills, held other important positions. They may have tooled precision machine parts used in tanks, devised better ways of delivering supplies to the front lines, or conducted research for the development of the atom bomb.

Women of that era joined the military, volunteered with the Red Cross, worked in defense plants and served on ration boards.

Once in a while I'm offered information for an obit about someone who served with another country's army during WWII. I rarely give these folks more than a sentence acknowledging their military service. Their military records may be impossible to locate.

Bobby Carse, an all-star professional hockey player and native Canadian, served with a Canadian army infantry division during WWII. Because his wartime experiences had been well documented, I was able to include them in his obituary in 1999.

On Oct. 12, 1944, Carse was with a handful of soldiers who were cornered in a farmhouse by German troops. He was shot in the right shoulder during the attack and taken prisoner.

Over the next six months, he was shifted from camp to camp and forced to march across Germany during the winter. Weakened by his wounds and malnutrition, he lost 60 pounds by the time he was liberated by the Allies in April 1945. He recuperated, was back on the ice in 1946 and went on to enjoy an illustrious hockey career.

I've received a few problematic requests from bereaved folks whose loved ones served with foreign armies. People in Eastern Europe often fought with or against monarchy loyalists and/or communist revolutionaries while German troops occupied their countries. Able-bodied men in places like Ukraine were drafted into Hitler's service against their will. Some served with the home guard, a police force controlled by the

Germans.

Whether a soldier is considered a patriot, a freedom fighter or an enemy depends on a person's point of view. We may have difficulty recognizing that our loved one was not on our nation's side.

A young man once called to ask me to write an obit for his late grandfather, who served in the Italian army and was a prisoner of war. I asked him, "Who was holding him prisoner? The Americans?"

He was speechless. Apparently, the fact that Italy was governed by Benito Mussolini, who was in cahoots with Adolf Hitler, never crossed the grandson's mind. He believed that his grandfather must have been captured by German troops and was held in a POW camp with William Holden's character from the movie, "Stalag 17." I instructed him to gather more details about Grandpa's wartime experience.

Another obit writer penned the old man's story, which turned out to be surprisingly interesting. Grandpa had been captured by American troops and sent to a prison camp in northern Ohio. He met his future wife when he and several other prisoners attended services at a Catholic church with a predominantly Italian congregation. Romance blossomed. Grandpa was sent back to Italy when the war ended, but soon returned to marry his sweetheart and settle in the States.

It's been reported that we're losing between 1,000 and 1,500 WWII veterans a day. That's probably true. Most of the veterans whose obits I've penned served in that war.

I haven't had as many opportunities to write obituaries for those who served in the prequel, World War I, the "War to End All Wars." Most of them have already gone on to their reward. Any who remain with us have to be centenarians by now.

© The Plain Dealer, May 22, 1995

KOREAN WAR POW APPEARED ON LIFE'S COVER; VINCENT SIMONETTI RETAINED HIS FAITH

By Alana Baranick, Plain Dealer Reporter

Cleveland Heights — The photograph of an unidentified captive soldier made the cover of Life magazine in 1951 and put a face on American troops captured during the Korean War.

It also informed the parents of Vincent G. Simonetti that their son, who had been reported missing in action, was alive. Mr. Simonetti's Army unit was sent to Korea in August 1950. In November, he was captured by Chinese soldiers who had cut off United Nations forces at the Changjin (Chosin) Reservoir.

A month later, before he was taken to Prisoner of War Camp No. 5, the exhausted, grimy 19-year-old, wearing summer fatigues and a parka in bone-chilling conditions, was looking up at American fighter planes overhead when someone snapped his picture. Although the photograph was credited to Life magazine photographer David Douglas Duncan, Mr. Simonetti recalled that a Chinese photographer took the picture.

A relative in Cleveland saw the picture on the cover of Life and told Mr. Simonetti's parents their son was alive. The photograph, titled "Christmas for a GI," was included in "The Best of Life" anthology printed in 1973.

Mr. Simonetti, 64, of Cleveland Heights, died Wednesday at Richmond Heights General Hospital after suffering a heart attack at the Richmond Mall.

His health problems started in the POW camp, where torture was routine and medical care non-existent. He and a dozen of his comrades were jammed into a tiny cell, where they slept in shifts stacked on top of each other. It was not unusual for a POW to wake up and find himself sleeping next to a friend who had died overnight.

During his 33 months in captivity, the Cleveland native shrank from 155 to 99 pounds. Hunger prompted him to steal food from enemy pantries at night and take it back to his fellow inmates, who dubbed him "The Shadow." Each of the 13 times he was caught, Mr. Simonetti was beaten, tied up and thrown into a pit.

When he was freed Aug. 20, 1953, a month after an armistice had been signed, he was suffering from malnutrition and nervous disorders caused by beriberi, a vitamin-deficiency disease.

During his imprisonment, Mr. Simonetti never lost his faith in God. He used his knuckles as rosary beads for counting prayers and often led his fellow Catholics in reciting the Mass, which he knew by heart.

Years later, he joined the Korean War Veterans and attended POW reunions, where he often renewed friendships with soldiers he had believed were dead. He also belonged to the American Legion.

His wartime experiences left lifelong scars of physical and mental pain. In 1960, Mr. Simonetti, who suffered arthritis of the spine, degenerative joints, angina, nightmares, crippling headaches and shortness of breath, was declared 50 percent disabled by the government.

When he could work, he stocked shelves, drove a truck, sold cars and repaired traffic signals for Cleveland Heights. He also lived and worked in Louisville, Ky., as an assistant branch manager of a development company for a short time in the early 1970s.

Survivors include his wife, Yolanda; sons, Charles J. of Cleveland Heights and Joseph J. of Cleveland; daughter, Landy M. Marine of Cleveland Heights; two grandchildren; three brothers; and two sisters.

Services will be at 10 a.m. today at St. Ann Catholic Church, 2175 Coventry Rd., Cleveland Heights.

DeJohn-Flynn-Mylott Funeral Home in South Euclid is in charge of arrangements.

Chapter 7

Tell Me Something Good

ALANA BARANICK

Once I've completed my research, I'm ready to interview family, friends, business associates or others who may help breathe life into the obit. I try to latch onto something that will make readers believe I knew the deceased or offer his friends never-before-seen glimpses into his life.

Earl H. Friess' obit would have been like any other for a man his age from his neighborhood — retired factory worker, World War II veteran, family man — had it not been for my interview with his son.

"So what did he do during the war?" I asked.

"He was in a German prison camp," his son said.

"Did he ever talk about what he did there?"

"Yes. He wrote poetry on the backs of cigarette packs."

Bingo!

With further questioning and info from his military discharge papers, I learned that Friess was serving with the Army Air Forces when the B-17 bomber on which he was a gunner was shot down over Mannheim, Germany. He was hit in the upper leg by shrapnel as he bailed out of the exploding aircraft. Although he used a parachute, the impact of the fall also caused his leg to break. The injuries left him with a permanent limp.

While imprisoned at a German prisoner-of-war camp, he wrote his poems on the unprinted sides of empty packs of Lucky Strikes, Camels and Chesterfields, which he compiled into booklet form. He dedicated it to American and English airmen "whose duty to our countries cannot be questioned."

Unlike police reporters, who have to deal with traumatized people who are often reluctant to talk about relatives who have been murdered or have taken their own lives, we obit writers interview bereaved folks who usually want to tell the world about their recently departed loved ones.

Nevertheless, they are grieving. They are fragile, and they have to be handled with care. Our mission is to make them feel comfortable, gain their confidence and convince them that we are on their side, while we extract the facts and hopefully walk away with some good quotes.

Voice and demeanor are important, even on the obit writer's telephone voice mail. My recorded voice provides callers, who are already annoyed that they're talking to a machine and not to a human being, with as much information as I can squeeze into the message. I give them my name, then tell them what day it is and that I'll be in the office until a specific time — not just "I'm either out of the office or not at my desk." Then I give them the appropriate fax number and email, as well as instructions for connecting with our newsroom telephone operators for assistance.

My natural tendency would be to end my message with "Have a nice day." But that is a ridiculous thing to say, when most of my callers are grieving over a death. So I close the recording with "Thank you for calling, and have a decent day."

When talking over the phone to a sobbing widow who can't see your face, think of yourself as a National Public Radio announcer. They've got such soothing, non-threatening voices, never whiny, loud, cold or rude.

After the opening amenities, I usually tell the relatives that I have some information for the obit, but that I need their help in filling in the blanks and in making sure I understand everything. I explain what we're going to do. I say, "Let me get some basics first, then you can tell me what you want me to know. And then I may have some more questions."

I get the facts first. I find that if I don't get the basics first, I might get caught up in the story and forget some crucial information. Then I let the bereaved loved ones ramble, sharing details about the deceased that I would never uncover through standard questions. After that, I might ask for more colors with which to paint the story of the person's life.

Sometimes the relative will say, "I think that's all I have to say." Other times, they ramble on and on about everything from why this fellow didn't serve in the military during World War II to what he had for breakfast on the day that he died.

When the interview is face-to-face, you have the added challenge of not only sounding sympathetic. You have to look the part. Shake the bereaved relative's hand, look at him with puppy-dog eyes and thank him for coming out of his way to bring a photo or whatever.

Be careful not to offend bereft folks who come to see you. If you're wearing a Grateful Dead T-shirt, turn it inside out before you go to the lobby to meet the people whose loved one is freshly dead. And take off those dangling skull earrings!

Words also can inadvertently offend. Be cautious in your phrasing. Think about what you say and how you say it. Don't say, "So was she just a housewife?" No woman is "just a housewife." Instead say, "So how did folks outside the family know your mom? Did she work outside the home? Did she do any volunteering? Did she belong to any organizations?"

Be honest with them, and subtly let them know you expect them to be honest with you.

Before I have a chance to find out how boring or exciting the deceased's life was, I tell the families that, although I hope to write their loved one's obit, I can't guarantee when or even if the obit will run. We have the time, space and resources to run a only few stories a day. It's best not to give them unrealistic expectations.

I also let them know that we regard the obits as news stories, not eulogies. So we might not include some things they want in the story. We might add other nifty things that they hadn't thought about or, in some cases, unflattering things they might not like. I explain that we do extensive research to corroborate what they tell us.

Don't be confrontational. Getting a bereaved relative mad is like making Bruce Banner angry. You wouldn't like him when he's angry. He might turn into a big, green, mean, monstrous Hulk.

This is especially true of young adult children who have lost a parent and haven't experienced the death of a loved one before. They act as though they have some kind of divine right to have the story done their way. It's as if they're saying, "How dare you portray my dad as anything less than saintly, when even as we speak he's moving into the mansion next door to Jesus?"

Reviewing the list of surviving relatives or which dead relatives are going to be mentioned in the obit can be a testy subject. I've been asked to include cats, dogs, daughters' best friends, next-door neighbors and hospice workers in the list of surviving relatives. Many families want to list foreign exchange students who lived with them for a year and kept in touch for the last 30 years as members of the immediate family.

My mantra is, "Come, let us reason together." First I ask them, "If we list a nonrelative as a surviving child, how would that person's true parent feel?" If that doesn't work, I bring up the genealogy issue, telling them that this would confuse future generations wanting to trace their lineage.

If all else fails, I say, "I'll do what I can to work them into the story, but they might be eliminated in the editing process."

LUKE SKYWALKER MAY NOT HAVE WANTED TO ADMIT that Darth Vader was his father in "The Empire Strikes Back," but by "Return of the Jedi," he was cool with it. I try to get grieving relatives to make a faster turn around when they initially object to having the truth printed in the deceased's obit. But it doesn't always work.

I encountered one seriously disturbed group who didn't want the mother of the dead man listed in his obituary. They wanted his stepmother listed as his mom. "They" were the deceased's siblings. It was their own mother they wanted blackballed from the obit, much the way she had been banished from their lives.

I don't know what really went on in that family to create such hostility on the part of the woman's children. It wasn't like she gave birth, then disappeared. She had raised her son. She and his father were divorced after their son was in college.

The mom calmly told me she had a good relationship with her son until his death. She gave up custody of her younger children to her wealthy ex-husband, who had a new wife and a big house. She believed he could offer them a better environment than what they would find in her small apartment while she completed her education and found work.

Two of her surviving children screamed at me in stereo on a conference call. If we had to list this woman, whom they despised, they said they didn't want their brother's obituary to be printed at all. Which was just fine with me. Oddly, those kids called me back a couple of days later to thank me for listening to them.

Give the bereaved time to talk it out and give them space to cry or yell. When they start choking up, tell them to take their time. You can wait. Don't rush them. When possible and when you can do it with sincerity, compliment the deceased. "What a nice guy he must have been. I wish I had known him." But don't say it if you don't mean it.

Offer your condolences to the grieving relatives. And be sure to thank them for taking time to talk about their loved one when they are so busy with funeral arrangements and such.

Try not to ask questions that can be answered with "Yes" or "No." When they say, "He was wonderful," I ask, "What made him wonderful?" If the deceased would "do anything for anybody," I ask, "What kind of things did he do for others?" If they say, "He was honest to a fault," I say, "Give me some examples of his honesty." Rule of thumb: Show, don't tell.

When I haven't snagged the life-breathing information I want, I like to ask, "What was it about your insert-relationship-here that set him apart from the rest of the crowd?"

Sometimes folks don't know how to respond to that. Some come up with something wonderful or pitiful. I once put that question to a widow about her husband. Her response was, "He had his faults." Then she said she didn't want to talk about him. I think that was just as well.

One man called to tell me about his late ex-wife. What was special about her? "She weighed 115 pounds when I met her, and she weighed 115 pounds when she died," he said with no concept of how awful that sounded. It's no wonder they were divorced.

IF YOU'RE LUCKY, YOU'LL FIND AN ARTICULATE PERSON with vivid memories that will make readers believe you personally knew the deceased. Comedic actor Tim Conway and other former students of retired high school English teacher Elsa Jane Carroll helped me achieve that goal when I penned her obituary in September 2002.

The elderly woman once turned down A&E's "Biography" producers' requests to interview her for their cable television show's segment on Conway. "I told her, 'I'd like you to do it. You are the most influential person in my life,' " Conway said to me by telephone from his home in California. "She said, 'But you're the one that did it.' "

Conway, best known for his television work on "The Carol Burnett Show" and "McHale's Navy," went on to explain how Carroll worked her magic on him.

"I was not interested in education; I was interested in horses," he said. "I wanted to be a jockey, if you could believe it. Then she gave me a term paper to write on Man o' War."

The assignment, to conduct research and compose a story about the legendary thoroughbred racehorse, turned Conway around. Using her trademark green ink, which several students told me about, Carroll marked his term paper with an "A," not because it was deserved, but because she wanted to encourage him, Conway contended.

"She inspired me to continue, to say, 'Gee! Reading and writing is not that bad.' It paid off," said Conway, whose written works include television material, film scripts and a book.

Other former students, some of whom were planning a memorial service for Carroll, called or emailed to add their two bits. One proclaimed, "If you made inquiries in Chagrin Falls, you would discover a consensus about who was the greatest high school teacher of the 20th century. That person would be Miss Elsa Jane Carroll."

Conway made a point of visiting her whenever he came back to Ohio. The last time he saw her was about six months before she died at age 95. "She was as spry and spunky as ever," he said.

In the part of the obit where we list the surviving relatives, I was able to say with confidence: "Carroll has no immediate family, but is survived by a host of former students who loved her."

WHISTLING WHILE SHE WORKED; MARY ANN HACKMAN, MOM TO 11, RAN AN EFFICIENT, HAPPY HOME

BY ALANA BARANICK, PLAIN DEALER REPORTER

Lyndhurst — Mary Ann Hackman sang happy ditties to the rhythm of her constantly running washing machine as she ran her one-woman peanut-butter-and-jelly-sandwich production line for her 11 kids and their friends.

The 73-year-old Lyndhurst resident, who died May 7 of leukemia, always sang, hummed or whistled while she worked.

"One baby over her shoulder, a stack of laundry in her arms, she'd bounce up the stairs singing, 'Up we go. Up we go,' " said her daughter, Ginny, a.k.a. Child No. 3. "She sang when she chopped baby food. She was just superb at multi-tasking, and she made it all look very easy."

Hackman often welcomed her children's friends and cousins to her home, then in University Heights, for sleepovers.

"I remember having my friends over, and we would play 'Island,' throwing all the furniture cushions on the floor and jumping from one to the other," said No. 7, Mary. "My mom would walk in and say, 'Hi, girls. Do you want a snack?' My friends could not get over this."

She even accommodated extra guests on family vacations at Linwood Park in Vermilion.

"One morning, on her 'vacation,' she made breakfast for 23 people - scrambled eggs and bacon and toast - and took the clothes to the Laundromat across the street," said Peggy Gillespie, No. 2. "She never yelled. Maybe she was just too tired."

If she was tired, she didn't let on. When her kids were tucked in for the night, she'd sit on their beds, play guitar and sing "Puff the Magic Dragon" or tell them stories about her childhood.

Then she'd put another load of clothes in the washer, pack

lunches for the next day and squeeze in a game of bridge with friends.

Hackman, who held a bachelor's degree in home economics, managed her time and her limited dollars efficiently.

Her brood ate dinner in shifts. She fed the younger ones in the kitchen before her husband, Gerry, came home from his purchasing job with the Cleveland schools. Then the rest of the family ate in the dining room.

To save money, Hackman sometimes sent Gerry out to buy several hamburgers and a few milkshakes that she poured into several smaller cups at home. She topped the burgers with cheese and baked frozen french fries to complete the feast.

Her firstborn, Gary, was 18 when she had her last child, Bill. When Bill started kindergarten, Hackman began a successful career in real estate sales.

"She was not some high-powered lady," said Paul, No. 9. "Her specialty was helping young couples get starter homes. Five or 10 years down the road, they'd go back to her and buy bigger homes."

Hackman, whose maiden name was Patterson, grew up in Cleveland Heights, the second of six children.

"She was always like a second mother to me," said her youngest sister, Barb. "We'd all go to her for advice. She seemed to know what to say."

As a teenager, Hackman worked as a playground instructor at Anthony Wayne School, where she organized games, taught crafts and read stories to elementary school children, like Alice Mathews.

"She was clever, fair, warm and gentle - almost a June Allyson quality," Mathews said. "As a result, I used to go to the playground every day, just because she was there. I felt a degree of importance because of how she treated me."

Hackman played a lot of tennis between pregnancies. She also enjoyed golf, fishing and bowling. In the 1990s, after she was widowed, she went kayaking in Alaska.

"She loved to read, loved a cold beer, loved going to Indians games and was a Browns fan," Mary said.

Hackman also found time to volunteer. She did laundry for a nursing home, picked up food for hunger centers and helped other people's children improve their reading skills.

She believed that every child was a blessing, never a burden.

Tell Me Something Good

Once, when she was polishing furniture, she stopped to admire a baby's hand print on the table. She showed it to Peggy and said:

"Isn't that adorable? I almost don't want to polish it away."

Chapter 8

The Goodbye Boy

Stephen Miller

This is the story of how I founded and ran an Internet magazine devoted to obituaries. It is the story of an obsession that led me to spend seven years chronicling the dead for no money and little fame.

Thanks to happenstance and dedication, I am today the obituaries editor of The New York Sun, a new version of the original "penny daily" newspaper that democratized newspapers in the first half of the nineteenth century.

GoodBye! - The Journal of Contemporary Obituaries (back issues still available at www.goodbyemag.com) was born of a long-standing writing habit seeking an outlet. In some ways it was a stunt, producing a 'zine that would satisfy me intellectually and allow me to show off to friends and family.

I was earning a good living as a technologist in a Wall Street bank, which bored me, as it does many others in the profession. I had a diverse background that included newspaper reporting and anthropological fieldwork, and as I contemplated the obituaries, I sensed a need. I found even the best American obituaries — those in the New York Times, for instance — unsatisfying. I decided to take a conventional form and twist it. I liked the idea of invigorating a hyperconventionalized form. I liked the creepiness of the enterprise: GoodBye! would be a magazine devoted to death.

It was not the first time I had written obits. In my days at the North Bergen Dispatch (a small New Jersey newspaper known to cognoscenti as

"The Disgrace" and now sadly deceased), I worked on the night rewrite desk. Among my duties was serving as an obituary recorder. "Recorder" because there was a form to fill out on the phone with an undertaker. It yielded the kind of obit I loathe, a scant five or six paragraphs that flattened a life into birth, education, matrimony, children, profession, and the like.

Obituaries like that made my mouth itch, even then. They were so wrong, so deadening of what any life represents, not only for the deceased, but also for the reader. Occasionally I mocked the form by inserting fake obituaries of my friends. One declared that my pal had been an upstanding scoutmaster. (He wasn't one.)

Years later, when I was casting about for a writing project, it occurred to me that mini-biographies could be occasions for humor, and even for short essays. In January 1996 I researched a number of recent deaths and sent them to friends as a Xeroxed newsletter.

GoodBye! took a while to gel. Early issues included more or less traditional obits reproduced from elsewhere, list-like compilations of deaths in fields like plastics and the arts, and even an April Fools obit of Gene Kelly that was completely fictional except that Kelly had died (I made him into a dentist-cum-spy).

Eventually I settled on a mix of utterly factual obits written and researched by myself and supplemented occasionally by other writers I could convince to write for me for free. The criteria for inclusion were that the individual must have died during the months on the masthead, and that the individual interested me.

GOODBYE! BEGAN AS A MONTHLY, became a bimonthly, and within a year settled into a quarterly. It varied in length between eight and 20 pages, featuring five to 10 major obituary essays. Regular sidebars included "Darwinian Events," self-inflicted removals from the gene pool, "Deaths of the Animals," and an annual feature of "Deaths 100 Years Ago," which I researched in microfilmed newspapers.

About a year after it first appeared, I put GoodBye! on the Web, and it is there that the magazine found a wider audience. People who read it on the Web wanted to read the printed version and many wanted to send it to their friends, so paid subscriptions emerged.

Even so, it was an expensive hobby. At the time, I did not agree with Dr. Johnson's quote, "No man but a blockhead ever wrote except for money." Now I do, sort of, but I always fantasized that my magazine would become a money maker.

I never came up with a business model that would support a magazine devoted entirely to obituaries. Who wants their business associated with death? Undertakers are not noted for their humor. The joie de vivre of death does not sit well with commerce.

Still, a lot of people are interested in obituaries. Not only did thousands read GoodBye! every month on the Web, but NPR, the Washington Post, and other publications in the US and abroad ran features on GoodBye!

ONE OF THE BEST THINGS about editing the Journal of Contemporary Obituaries was the correspondence I received:

"Me and my friends are fighting about whether Mr. T is dead. I swear I heard it last summer on the news. I know this link didn't say 'if you wanna find out if Mr. T is dead click here,' but could you help me out?"

"Would you please tell me the name of the English actor who recently died? I think his first name was Peter."

On the death of Gene Siskel: "You forgot to mention what we all wanna know. Is he a fag? Sorry, was?"

I got intriguing commercial propositions: "Can you use a good distributor in South America?"

On the death of a Beatles' wife: "I think you are an asshole for what you say about Linda McCartney. Wow, like you have ever contributed anything to this world?"

Followers of the Church of Satan were among my most persistent critics. When my obit of Anton LaVey, founder of the "church," appeared in the November 1997 issue, it caused an outpouring of bile. It was a glorious thing for a 'zine publisher:

"You fail to see the reasoning behind the rhyme of LaVey's definition of 'evil.' Satanists themselves represent many things, but we are far from the hypocritical religions which spawned us. We believe in banality, carnal bliss and joy in life, not waiting for some intangible paradise.

"Ave Satanas."

I also got a lot of mail from people looking for relatives. Most of these I referred to local dailies or libraries. My favorite is this one:

"Where do I have to look to find out if my ex-husband, who lives in Florida or Ohio, is dead? I haven't heard a word from him in ten years and with the lifestyle he leads I'm sure he's probably dead by now."

WHEN I STARTED GOODBYE!, I thought that a critical approach, warts and all, would be much more interesting than hagiography. Liberal amounts of humor would be part of the mix, too. I had no idea that the British had thought of some of my best ideas first.

It was a revelation to me when a friend returned from London with a paperback edition of London Daily Telegraph obits. They were hilarious and compulsively readable.

GoodBye! followed the British model of laughing at the proud and including as much scandalous detail as possible. For instance, in the obituary of former far-right-wing Congressman John Schmitz, GoodBye! included the clinical details of the child abuse case which led to his being outed as an adulterer and father of two children with a mistress. And his downfall.

His legitimate daughter, a teacher named Mary Kay Letourneau, also became scandalously famous. She went to jail for raping a 12-year-old student and was caught screwing him again in her car after being paroled. She had two daughters with him. The teacher and her former student later married.

GoodBye! elaborated on the British model with the idea that the traditional rosters of vital statistics can be passed by altogether. In many cases, the existence of a corpse served as an inspiration for an essay that pretty much omitted the decedent's life course, outside of a few major achievements. The main constraints were the name of the decedent and facts.

What did this mean in practice?

The Goodbye! obit for Alex Comfort did not start with a death sentence, telling readers when, where and at what age the author of the graphically illustrated book, The Joy of Sex, died. Instead, it began:

"Paging through the 1972 bestseller The Joy of Sex isn't like the carnal epiphanies of a stroke book. It's more like a recipe book for decent, solid cuisine that doesn't make you salivate - like the old Joy of Cooking whose title was its inspiration. But Alex Comfort's prose is much wittier than that of the Rombauers,"(the Joy of Cooking authors).

The GoodBye! obituary continues with an extended comparison between the two works:

"Both books feature memorable drawings. The Joy of Cooking (in my grandmother's 1953 edition) has stylized depictions of a female hand in the act of making cookies, rolling out a pie crust, skinning a squirrel, and plunging spaghetti into a boiling pot. The Joy of Sex features a female hand pumping her lover's manhood into a second erection."

After more of this it moves to a brief biography, then back to Comfort's philosophy of sex, and finally an evaluation of what his work meant for its readers.

In a daily newspaper, the obituarist's obligation is to present some facsimile of a complete record of the person's life. So the Times found space to print excerpts from the reviews of Comfort's early novels and gerontological work. But too much detail kills the buzz. In GoodBye!, obituaries could be funny, compelling, and tell deeper truths.

GoodBye! often omitted causes of death, or age at death, and lists of survivors. So what? What mattered was the reader's experience. Or, I admit, the writer's amusement.

Carolyn Gilbert, a person of immense vision who had taken it upon herself to organize the world of obituary writers into an annual conference, invited me to address her Third Great Obituaries Writers Conference, located at the unlikely town of Las Vegas, N.M., and I obliged with a paper that I thought would blow the socks off conventional obituary writers nationwide. I ended my conference address with the following:

"Americans have traditionally been somewhat loathe to address life's end. The historian Arnold Toynbee wrote that 'death is un-American, an affront to every citizen's inalienable right to life, liberty, and the pursuit of happiness.' 'Do not speak ill of the dead,' is a chestnut dear to the American breast."

But we must speak ill of the dead, and we must speak well of them too. If we are to learn from the dead, or enjoy their lives in a meaningful way, we must speak of them freely, think of them objectively and creatively, and report on them with honesty and fervor and humor. This honors their memory better than an idealistic, bureaucratic laundry list.

I have now moved on to writing and editing the obituaries section in a daily newspaper in New York City, where I have the great privilege of burying the famous for a larger audience. Some of my theories about bending the form have paled in the face of the daily grind of stiffs and the necessity of presenting a more holistic view of the dead to an audience, some of whom actually knew them. This has in some ways vitiated my optimistic ideas of a new world of obituaries. At the same time, I believe I brought a new sensibility to the form, and at least introduced to the New York audience a great new place to read about the dead.

GoodBye!, if it is not dead, is at least in a vegetative state, still available on the Web as long as I keep the Web site open. I still get email from readers about its more inflammatory decedents - a recent exchange about porn star Linda Lovelace stands out in memory - but I've gone legit, sold out. I have had a son in the interim, and I don't have the time to keep GoodBye! current. GoodBye! will always represent for me an ideal, the thing that the obits could be.

GoodBye! The Journal of Contemporary Obituaries,
July-September 2002

THE GOSPEL OF PASTRY

BY STEPHEN MILLER

Consider the frosted doughnut. It does not sell itself.

It is a curiosity, perhaps even a confirmation of Max Weber's thesis in The Protestant Ethic and the Spirit of Capitalism, that successful franchisers tend to take on the aspect of a revival preacher. Their gospel is one of salvation through efficient workplaces. Jesus instructed the faithful to render unto Caesar what is Caesar's. William Rosenberg said to render unto the customer whatever the customer wanteth, especially when it comes to doughnuts.

He was one of the first great preachers of the gospel of management, and his words found fertile soil. Temples to his vision, Dunkin' Donuts, litter the landscape like revival tents. Customers make their morning obeisances of coffee and crullers at more than 5,000 franchised chapels throughout this land and in 37 other countries.

Thus sayeth Rosenberg: "A person does not build a business; a person builds an organization." And further: "The customer is the boss." Heed his words: "Good enough is never good enough, is it?" "Show me a person who never made a mistake and I will show you a person who never did anything." One of his parables: "Consider the fragile snowflake that flutters slowly to earth and disintegrates; however, if enough of them stick together they can paralyze an entire city." Finally his charge to the congregation: "Make time for doughnuts."

Rosenberg was born, much like another man with a message, a Jew in straitened circumstances. He grew up in suburban Boston. As a young man in the Depression, he dropped out of school and delivered groceries and telegrams for Western Union. One summer day he dragged a block of ice to the racetrack to sell cracked ice to hot race fans and made $171 in one night, a small fortune for a poor adolescent. When he was 21 he was national sales manager for Jack and Jill, a New England ice cream company. After working in a shipyard during WWII, he cashed in war bonds and borrowed from relatives to start a business selling food at work sites from trucks and taxis fitted with stainless-steel shelves. His Industrial Luncheon Service was his first great marketing ministry. Within a few years he

75

was running nearly 200 trucks around New England and in New York. Then he ran in-plant cafeterias and vending machines.

Soon, he received another series of revelations: revenues from the trucks came mainly from sales of coffee and pastries. Taking inspiration from Howard Johnson's, and its 28 flavors, he opened a stand-alone store that offered 52 varieties of doughnuts, one for each week of the year. Like any great religious leader, he thus linked his liturgy to the progression of the seasons. Although the first shop was called "Open Kettle," by 1950 it was named "Dunkin' Donuts." By 1954 there were five shops, and the next year he started franchising the operation as a way of bringing in new capital. As with many religions, franchising was once considered a scourge, and was borderline illegal in many communities. Would that the wisdom of those elders had not gone unheeded; thanks to Rosenberg and his fellow pioneers at McDonald's and Kentucky Fried Chicken, the nation's palate has become depressingly uniform. The International Franchise Association that he founded in 1960 now counts some 30,000 members.

By the early 1960s he was rolling in - well - dough, not ceasing his hard-baking ways but easing off enough to purchase a stable in New Hampshire, which quickly became the largest producer of pacers in New England. Meanwhile his doughnut fortunes - well - rose as he took the company public, overcame multiple cancers, took his sons into the business, started selling so-called bagels, and generally insinuated himself so completely into life in America, at least, that one can only hope there is some vulnerable point in this happy pastry death star that will destroy it completely with one shot. Of course not.

Rosenberg died at 86, still happily consuming his own product, apparently not killed by it, and still professing the gospel of the doughnut.

When interviewed recently by a peevish Chicago anchorwoman who insisted that his product would condemn the nosher's soul, or at least his heart, to a fatty perdition, Rosenberg adopted the aspect of the Latin poet Terence, who urged, Ne quid nimis, or "Moderation in all things:" "Why ma'am, there's nothing in these but eggs, flour, butter, and a little sugar. Nothing in them will hurt you a bit. Just don't eat a box of them is all."

Chapter 9

A Place at the Sun

Stephen Miller

In New York City in 2003, a newspaper war helped create the first new metropolitan daily obituaries page in at least a generation. As part of its ceaseless process of self-reinvention, The New York Sun hired me to write and edit the obituaries, and to do it with panache. This chapter is the story of how it happened, and how it turned out.

Although the morals of the story turn out to be surprisingly conventional ones — write well, verify the spelling of the stiff's name, try to understand who your publisher's friends are — the details are piquant. For instance:

The Sun became the first newspaper (so far as I know) to have published the obituary of a fish.

The Sun blazed the path in stand-alone, "wild art" obituaries, in which details of the decedent's life are reduced to an extended photo cutline.

The Sun, unlike its uptown rival with the inflated reputation, never blatantly stole from another newspaper and then published an obituary of a person who was not even dead.

Readers, it's a bare-knuckle tussle, a rollicking, no-holds-barred set-to in New York journalism, although the obituaries sections are slightly more genteel. 'Twas ever thus, I wish!

In 2002, for the first time in many years, the New York Sun fired the first shot in a newspaper war. The previous war had ended in 1995, with the withdrawal of New York Newsday, the Long Island newspaper that had tried to launch a tony tab meant to clean the clocks of the Times, the Daily News, and the New York Post. New York Newsday tried to be upmarket of the News and Post, and more street-savvy than the Grey Lady. To many journalism fans, it succeeded brilliantly. To the Tribune Co., which controlled the budgets, it failed.

By 2002, a group of investors headed by editor Seth Lipsky, veteran of The Wall Street Journal and The Jewish Daily Forward took aim at the Times. The new paper would be a broadsheet, and editorially it would be well to the right of the Times, if not Genghis Khan. The paper was conceived as an outlet for neoconservative thought, for sophisticated cultural coverage, and for a thoughtful take on the news of the day.

In this way, it resembled the old New York Sun, a venerable, if dormant, newspaper name.

Ben Day founded the New York Sun in 1831 as the first of the so-called penny dailies, whose number would soon include the Herald, the Tribune, and decades later, the New-York Daily Times. Among the highlights of its history were the "Great Moon Hoax" of 1835, in which the paper published a series of articles claiming that powerful telescopes had spotted winged "bat-men" on the lunar surface and the "Yes, Virginia, there is a Santa Claus" letter.

The litany of The Sun's all-star content providers included Don Marquis, creator of Archie and Mehitabel; and Rube Goldberg. By the 1870s, the Sun, under editor Charles Dana, had established a reputation for savvy, witty, and somewhat conservative journalism.

As the great wave of newspaper mergers continued, the Sun was folded into the World-Telegram in 1950, and that newspaper went under during the great newspaper strike of 1967. By 2002, when the Sun was revived, pretty much the only things that remained of its 137-year history were a copper-green clock and a thermometer hung ostentatiously from the old Sun office building, on Broadway across the street from City Hall. The new offices were just a block away, and Lipsky's dream included reviving the stylish conservatism that had marked Dana's editorial tenure.

MY PACKAGE OF CLIPS happened to cross Managing Editor Ira Stoll's desk at a time when he had been thinking about starting an obituary section. In its first year of operation, The Sun had experimented with many sorts of features, and gone through multiple redesigns, and a slight shrinkage of the front page. There was a biography-of-the-week feature that was eventually canned, a feature called Smarter Times that corrected errors of fact and emphasis in the Times, sports columns, and other features that went away. The slogan changed from "New York on Page One" to

"Illuminate Your World." The editors were involved in multiple concept tweaks all at once, and my obits sections would be the latest.

Stoll had cleverly noted that the Times was neglecting local obituaries and concentrating on national deaths - he wanted a locally focused section. I wasn't barred from writing about people with no New York connection, but I should strive for the local angle. Also, he wanted news. The corpse should be no colder than two weeks, maximum.

"I could hire a couple of kids right out of J school, but you have a positive passion for this," Stoll told me, evidently astonished.

In a separate interview, editor Seth Lipsky, somber as an undertaker, growled, "This may not work. You may be just a plain reporter in six months." Then, glancing at one of my clips, a feature story on obituaries in New York newspapers in the 1850s, he proceeded to fill me in on the biography of Charles Dana, who had served as President Lincoln's personal war reporter during the Civil War before assuming the editorship of The Sun, in 1869. I found it greatly comforting that he cared as much for history as I did. "You're an interesting young man," he said gently. "Now get to work."

Going into the job, I knew that my biggest challenge would be to find out who was dead. At an established newpaper with an established obituaries section, an editor might sit back and wait for applicants. Indeed, when I asked the late Richard "Noodle" Pearson, editor of the Washington Post's exemplary obituary page, what to expect, he told me that my biggest problem would be fighting off grieving relatives and explaining why I wasn't running certain obituaries. Carolyn Gilbert, head of the International Association of Obituarists, urged me to put into writing a formal set of guidelines concerning who qualified.

I had worked on the night desk at various dailies in New Jersey, and I was used to the routine of funeral directors calling up to submit obituaries, so I was surprised to find out that that in New York things were different. New York, unlike many states, has laws protecting the privacy of the deceased that prevent funeral directors from releasing information, and I was surprised to find that most wouldn't even talk to me. When I faxed an introductory note to about 30 funeral homes, I got zero response. Hospitals in general couldn't release information unless the family specifically requested them to, and the coroner's office was no help at all. I intended to create an obituary section like no other, but I didn't expect to find that no one wanted to help me memorialize the dead.

I found other sources. Luckily, most newspapers have free websites, and I frequently find people in them who have died outside of New York who have had interesting lives that intersected the city. Another great source is the New York Times's own death notices, the agate type paid notes beneath the news obits. While these notices are for the most part dry and terse (the Times extracts a princely ransom for them) they contain pearls for a careful reader.

And so, after a week of preparation, the Sun ran its first obituary on February 24, 2003.

The lede went:

"For some men it would be enough to found and develop a large agricultural business, to invent a kind of kitty litter, to raise a family and, in the fullness of time, to retire from business to run a farm, raising horses and organic cattle. That man would be somebody other than George Plitt, who did those things, but also had a hobby: teaching his rooster to roller skate."

I grimace a little when I read that, and I'll come back to why a little later.

Running next to Plitt's 1,200-word tombstone was a photo that set the tone for the page nicely: a smiling middle-aged gent hefting a shotgun, with his foot on a grouse he'd plugged. He was in the happy hunting grounds now, for sure.

I doubt anybody at the Times even noticed that The Sun had initiated an obits page (and to my consternation The Sun ran no announcement).

ALTHOUGH MOST OF THE NEW YORK DAILIES ran obituaries, and a writer for the New York Post even won a Pulitzer for one in the early 1960s, the obituary as a valorized form did not catch on until Alden Whitman began interviewing famous people "for later," as he tactfully put it. Whitman, an eccentric who affected a French police inspector's cape, did great work and helped establish the Times as the best place to be caught dead in. His obituaries were anthologized in books. Whitman retired in 1976, and the Times continued to set the standard.

In the 1990s another excellent writer emerged on its obituary page: Robert McG. Thomas. Thomas concentrated his talents on eccentrics, and attracted admirers with his flip style. After he died in 2000, a line in his obituary ran, "Robert McGill Thomas Jr. was born and grew up in Shelbyville, Tenn., where chopped liver is rare and schmaltz is not part of the vernacular." It was a very Thomas-esque line, and the kind of flourish that would become rarer at the Times with his departure. Some of Thomas's gems were collected in the book "52 McG's," and one of these concerned Edward Lowe, who invented kitty litter.

Well so, his family told me, did George Plitt. Both inventions occurred in the 1940s. Further research showed that neither Plitt's Kitty Kleen nor Lowe's Tidy Kat was patented, so the whole question of priority is, as I suggested in the obit, "destined for the ash heap of history." Doubtless, there is a complicated history of kitty litter going back to the Egyptians to be written by some polymathic egghead ("Kitty Litter: The odor-fighting grains that changed the world"). Suffice to say that I was pleased by the symbolic challenge to the Times, even if I was the only one in the world who understood its full ramifications.

THE FIRST FEW WEEKS AT THE SUN WERE PAINFUL, yet exciting. The Prime Minister of the small South Pacific nation Nauru happened to die while visiting New York, and I used the occasion to enlighten Sun readers about the ecological devastation the island had suffered by literally bulldozing itself into a moonscape while mining guano, bird droppings that are used for fertilizer.

Then there was the fish obit. The fish died — it was a long-term denizen of an upstate diner, and when it sickened a few weeks before death, sentimental customers had fitted it with a buoyancy harness. After I ran an obit for a former Kentucky Derby winner who had perished a few weeks later, I was implored to banish non-human species from the Sun's obits, and so, sadly, I have.

Stand-alone, "wild art" obituaries, in which details of the decedent's life are reduced to an extended photo cutline, are part of my obit-writing arsenal. Sometimes a picture tells the story better than a written obituary could, especially when the subject is a Hollywood starlet. I love running a fleshy photo of a forgotten babe of yesteryear.

When Mickey Deans, Judy Garland's fifth and last husband, died in 2003, I ran a photo of them cutting their wedding cake with this extended cutline that served as Deans' obit:

"WEDDING BELL BLUES - Judy Garland, 47, and nightclub manager Mickey Deans, 35, were wed in London on March 15, 1969. It was her fifth and final marriage, his first. A London columnist described their empty reception as 'the saddest and most pathetic party I have ever attended.' Three months later she was dead of an overdose of barbiturates. Deans, whose real name was Michael DeVinko, died last Friday in Cleveland after a long illness, at age 68. Originally a pianist and singer, he managed the fashionable New York nightclub Arthur in the late 1960s, where the two met. After Garland's death, Deans wrote a memoir of their time together titled 'Weep No More My Lady.' In the book, Garland comes off as vain and insecure, yet loving and dignified. He struggles to prop up her sagging career. Deans dropped out of the public eye, eventually moving to Cleveland. There, he operated an entertainment production company and purchased a local landmark, a reputedly haunted 19th century castle, which he attempted to restore."

Meanwhile, the stiffs were rolling in - authors, scientists, mountain climbers, jazz musicians and singers, showgirls, tycoons, basically anybody who had done anything the public noticed for any period was within the Sun's ambit.

I get more requests now, but the majority I find myself. I have jettisoned the former requirement that we won't run obits that the Times has run already. Now I only kill obits if the Times has done a really great job that I can't improve on.

Because New York is the center of the nation's theater, media, publishing, business and finance, and many other pursuits, the pickings are amazing.

THE WEEK OF JULY 11, 2003 HAD BEEN A GOOD ONE for obituaries in the New York Sun. Monday kicked the week off with Frances Rees, an activist who stopped a big power plant on the Hudson in the 1960s, an important victory in the history of environmentalism. Next came Herbert Weissberg, "Herbert, King of Gramercy," a well-known hotelier whose guests were among the few privileged souls allowed to visit Gramercy Park, escorted by the key-bearing doorman. Wednesday chronicled the life of David Loeb, founder of Countrywide, the largest independent mortgage backer in the nation, who had to leave New York to find financing to fund his country and make it literally nationwide. Thursday's obit was the longest of the week at 1,500 words - as long as the Sun ever goes on obits-not-for-the-Pope. It chronicled the life of Briggs Swift Cunningham, an endurance racer and heir to part of the Proctor & Gamble fortune, who founded a racing car company. "So identified was he with auto racing that when he won the America's Cup yachting competition in 1958, he made it sound almost like he had done it by accident," went the obit. "One does not win the America's Cup by accident."

On Thursday I found myself searching for somebody to round out the week, and finally fell upon one Priscilla Vail, an author and educator concerned with dyslexia, whose death notices had been running at length in the Times for a couple of days. It seemed like the kind of feel-good story that would end the week on a positive note. Meanwhile, it seemed like it would be quick and easy - my thoughts were frankly as much on getting up to the Catskills for the weekend as they were to memorializing a Connecticut educator.

Here's the lede for a story that I am ashamed to say bored me:

"Patricia Vail, a specialist in learning disabilities who wrote many books about how to facilitate child education, died of cancer July 6. She was 71.

"Among her books were the 'Homework Heroes' series, which provides advice for parents trying to help their children do homework; several about how to teach reading, and 'About Dyslexia: Unraveling the Myth.'"

Nothing seemed amiss until I got back to work Sunday and got a message from her son, whom I'd interviewed. He was pissed. Amusingly, he was just as aggravated that I had called her a Vassar dropout (as she was) as he was that I had committed the second-most serious sin that an obituarist can commit: I had gotten her name wrong.

Look back a couple of grafs. I found the death notice of Priscilla Vail, but I wrote the obit of Patricia Vail. My only excuse is that I used the right name at the end of the obit and my proofreaders failed to catch the error, too. But this one was really bad. I apologized to the son, published a correction, and thanked the deities that the Sun at the time had little circulation in Connecticut.

HANK BOROWY WAS A PITCHER for the Yankees in the 1940s who went on to have an interesting career with the Cubs in which he, among other achievements, managed to lose the 7th game of the last World Series the perpetually losing Chicago team managed to contend in, in 1945. When I found out, thanks to an obit via the Associated Press, that Borowy had expired, I called everyone I could think of to get some details. I didn't bother with the Yankees, because from experience I knew that they wouldn't be helpful, and I had no idea how to contact the Cubs. Finally, I found the funeral home in New Jersey that was handling the corpse - funeral homes in New Jersey will talk to you, unlike funeral homes in New York - but the director there told me the family was at the wake. I knew the Times would have him in the next day's paper. What to do?

Luckily, I have access to ProQuest, a monumental database of newspaper clips. Of course, as a pitcher for a major league baseball team, there were literally thousands of clips, but since I knew from the AP story what some of the important dates were - the World Series in which he had pitched, most saliently — I was able to cobble together a good account of Borowy's achievements.

By following up on various clues in those clips, I found that the Yankees' young and impetuous owner, Larry McPhail, dealt Borowy to another team in 1945 at a time when he was the ace of the staff. The deal caused a huge controversy that ended up changing baseball's waiver rules. Apparently the manager of the Yankees, Joe McCarthy, just didn't like him.

The Yankees failed to make the World Series that year by a few games, while Borowy won 21 games, the first pitcher to win over 20 pitching in both leagues. Yet he went 2-2 in the World Series and effectively lost the title for the Cubs. It was a great story, one that I was able to cobble together from clips.

Borowy had his best season by far in 1945 and after a few years retired. He became a real estate agent in his hometown of Bloomfield, N.J., and apparently did nothing else newsworthy in his life.

The moral of the story is that it is possible to write an interesting obituary using archival sources if you are persistent and lucky.

I get scooped constantly. Families of famous people call the Times when they croak. The reasons are, essentially, reputation and circulation. The Times sells a million copies a day, the Sun five percent of that. And the Times is THE place to die.

One day early on in my tenure, I was reprimanded for having stated in a public forum that "nobody reads us yet," a dumb thing to say in public, although I was furious at the British paper that reported it. The Sun's obituary section was an inviting target to that British paper because Conrad Black, the publisher of the competing London Daily Telegraph, also happened to be one of the Sun's backers.

THE GEORGE PLITT OBIT HAD A FINE, FEATUREY LEDE, but I wouldn't write it that way today. So far as I'm concerned, the lede should include the name and age of the deceased and the fact that he is deceased. Rich Pearson of the Washington Post once said, "Everyone dies in the first graph of my stories, but I console myself with the thought that there are relatively few complaints from people I write about."

When I published a quarterly obits 'zine, I abjured hackneyed writing and approached each decedent with the ambition of making his or her death an occasion for an interesting essay. But I found that a daily obituary section, which is reporting news, needs formulas. Daily journalism is different from magazine journalism. I believe that a news article needs to state right up front what the news is. The trick to making it interesting is to make the lede simple, factual, and if you are ambitious, eloquent and thematic.

Here is a fun one:

"Fay Wray, who died Sunday at age 96, long survived her tense affair with King Kong, and despite distinctly mixed feelings in the early days, came to love the great beast. A veteran of nearly 100 films, she is destined to be remembered almost solely as Ann Darrow, the screaming heroine of the 1933 film."

These two sentences touch nearly every theme in the 1,200-word obit, and they also add a note of dignity to the odd spectacle.

Most published obits for the movie star started something like this: "Fay Wray, who played opposite a giant ape that carried her to the top of the Empire State Building in the classic 1933 film King Kong, died Sunday at her Manhattan apartment at age 96."

Notice one subtlety typical of most American obituaries: the decedents' achievements are parenthetical to the fact that they have died — and the verb "died," which constitutes the reason for the story, is far removed from the subject. This gets the obituary exactly inside-out. The reason for the story is the death, and so it belongs near the subject; but the point of the story is the biography, so it is not parenthetical.

After the lede, I like to use a billboard, that is, summarize as sexily as possible what is most worth saying. Hence for Wray:

"'At the premiere of 'King Kong' I wasn't too impressed. I thought there was too much screaming,' she once said. 'I didn't realize then that King Kong and I were going to be together for the rest of our lives, and longer.'

"The film has assumed iconic status in the roster of American cinema, being regularly cited by academics, cineastes, and anyone else interested in watching a 40-foot gorilla fall in love while battling biplanes, pterodactyls, and a tyrannosaur.

"Yet in 1938, when newspapers across the country ran headlines detailing the breakup of Wray's first marriage, it was such films as 'Viva Villa,' 'The Wedding March,' and 'The Affairs of Cellini' that buttressed her reputation.

"Decades later, when the protagonist of 'The Rocky Horror Picture Show' sang 'Whatever Happened to Fay Wray?' viewers knew her solely as King Kong's screaming woman. What had happened to Fay Wray was that she had retired from acting, and her career had mutated in the culture's memory. 'At the present time, when I have decided to let the acting go and write a play, it is Kong who seems to function as my Public Relations Man,' Wray wrote in 1969. 'I no longer make any effort to escape.'"

From here, the obituary moves into several hundred words of chronological biographical exposition. Many obituary writers seem to feel that what is required is some kind of list of major achievements, but I think that achievements are more interesting when they are linked to a chronological format that gives the sense of a life being lived in time, where the decedent doesn't necessarily know what's coming.

In the daily format, the artistry is in things like the selection of detail and the connections between the paragraphs that give the reader the sense of a whole life lived under a broad theme introduced early in the piece.

The important thing here is depth and selection, and to make a good selection I have to do a lot of research quickly. I utilize used-book stores, online clips of newspapers, interviews, and anything else I can think of. Anything you can do to increase your knowledge of the stiff will produce a better story, and that's what matters: the experience of the reader.

By reader, I don't mean the family. There is nothing finer than receiving a note from a family member informing you that your obituary has caught the "real" decedent, but this is not the goal. Obituaries are not about giving each life its due. They are not about who deserves to get in the paper.

The goal is producing a piece of writing that is compelling — a factual biography that is a fun thing to read that will make the reader want to come back and check to see who's dead tomorrow. That's why I read, and that's what puts bread in my kid's mouth.

RICHARD NEY, 87, STAR OF 'MRS. MINIVER' AND PUGNACIOUS FINANCIAL WRITER

By STEPHEN MILLER, STAFF REPORTER OF THE SUN

Richard Ney, who died Sunday at age 87, was known to Wall Street denizens as the crusading investor who wrote "The Wall Street Jungle" to expose the role of specialist traders whom he claimed were rigging the markets; to movie fans he will always be Vin Miniver, the heroic young fighter pilot in "Mrs. Miniver" (1942), starring Greer Garson.

Not only did Garson win an Academy Award for her steely performance, but as a result of playing Mrs. Miniver she became Mrs. Ney. The 1943 wedding of Hollywood's hottest star to the man who had played her son — he was only two years her junior, according to the marriage license — made headlines. In newspaper photos of the newlyweds, Ney, who was by then serving under Admiral Halsey in the Aleutians, is wearing his ensign's uniform, and he looked, as always, dashing.

"Mrs. Miniver" is the story of a woman keeping her family together in the face of the London Blitz; the Garson-Ney alliance was less solid, and their union barely outlasted the war. At the divorce trial, Garson broke down while testifying that Ney had told her she was "finished as an actress" and complained about her age — she was in fact 13 years his senior.

Yet it was Ney who foundered, and after facing diminishing roles and failing as a Broadway musical producer, he switched careers and found great success as an investment adviser. After making an early splash in 1962 by predicting in Time that the stock market would crash (it did), he developed theories about how specialist traders cause stock prices to rise and fall. Ney made a pile of money trading on this basis, testified before the Senate about the role of specialists, and then wrote three best-sellers about his theories, which caused him to be vilified by many on Wall Street.

Ney was born in the Bronx and grew up in Harlem in poverty, living on his own by the time he was 15. He recalled earning pocket money by ironing and reselling used scorecards at ballparks, a story just bizarre enough to be true.

A youthful romance with a substitute high school art teacher led to his first marriage, soon dissolved. Her lasting effect on Ney was to convince him to study hard; he was accepted at Columbia, where he majored in economics and supported himself by modeling for Lord & Taylor's.

After graduation, Ney found a job at the 1939 World's Fair. He later claimed he was fired when he came up with a cliched-sounding slogan, according to his widow, Mei-Lee Ney. Literally walking the streets of Manhattan in search of work, Ney happened upon an audition for a production of "Life With Father," wangled himself a part, and soon found himself on a yearlong tour headlined by Dorothy Gish. His lack of acting experience was apparently an asset in his portrayal of the awkward character Clarence.

Ney claimed he was fired when he asked the producers for a weekly raise of $25. On a lark, he traveled to Hollywood with a friend, a French teacher who had found work teaching English to Michele Morgan for the production of "Joan of Paris" (1942). An agent who was casting "Mrs. Miniver" spotted Ney at the studio, and he was recruited more or less on the spot.

"Mrs. Miniver" had been intended by MGM as a modest film, but with American participation in World War II at full bore, the White House pressed for a wider release, surmising that its message of solidarity amid the bombs would be inspirational. (Years later, the Queen Mother supposedly told Garson,"We had no idea we were quite so brave.")

Ney soon found work in another patriotic film, "The War Against Mrs. Hadley" (1942), in which he played a bibulous ne'er-do-well transformed into a war hero. The film opened in Washington, D.C., with a "bond premiere" that sold more than $1 million in war bonds.

Ney then left to serve in the Navy, where part of his duty was helping sailors write letters home. He and Garson were married in haste while he was on leave, and they seem not to have co-habited for long. Ney reputedly found it uncomfortable living with Garson's mother in their home.

After their divorce, Ney had featured roles in "The Late George Apley" (1947) and "Ivy" (1947), in which he played Jervis Lexton, Joan Fontaine's doubly cuckolded husband. His roles got smaller and came less frequently. Eventually, he took work in Europe, appearing in "Miss Italia" (1950) as the romantic foil to a 23-year-old Gina Lollobrigida, which must have been thrilling. His final film, "Babes in Baghdad" (1952), starring Paulette Goddard and Gypsy Rose Lee, was meant to be an atmospheric harem romp; it was a failure. Ney recalled it as his worst film, although he fondly recalled his (platonic) friendship with the vivacious Goddard.

Ney next wrote the lyrics and book of a musical, "Portofino," in which the devil and a priest contest amidst an international auto race. The show, which he produced, made it to Broadway in the winter of 1958, but closed after just three performances to remarkably savage reviews. "I will not say that 'Portofino' is the worst musical ever produced because I have only been seeing musicals since 1919," wrote Walter Kerr of the Herald Tribune. Brooks Atkinson and the rest piled on, although Ney gamely attempted to showcase it again the next fall in San Diego.

Ney would later tell friends that the debacle was good for him because it convinced him to get out of show business and into the stock market. His lingering Hollywood cachet helped bring him attention, and after Time quoted him as the only one of its financial advisers to correctly predict the crash of 1962, his business skyrocketed. He produced a biweekly market newsletter that he used to propagate his ideas about the corrupt practices of trading specialists — and how to time them to the investor's advantage. In "The Wall Street Jungle," he wrote, "Hidden behind the facade of pompous jargon and noble affections, there is more sheer larceny per square foot on the floor of the New York Stock Exchange than any place else in the world."

Two more best-sellers followed, "The Wall Street Gang" (1974) and "Making It in the Market" (1975), about how to put his insights into operation. Later, he had a daily market roundup television program,"The Ney Report," on a financial television station in Los Angeles, KWHY.

Despite his skepticism about the honesty of the markets, he had no compunctions about making a good living off them, although he told the Los Angeles Times in 1968, "It's all pure and simple gambling."

He posed for the cover of "The Wall Street Jungle" behind the wheel of his midnight blue Rolls Royce, which he bought in London in the 1950s. He collected art, and treasured a Degas canvas. He ate sensibly, urged rice bran extract on friends as an elixir, and adhered to the vitamin regimen of Gaylord Hauser, the nutrition guru he knew through one of his old Hollywood friends, Greta Garbo.

He continued with his investment work virtually to the last day of his life, and continued to be a contrarian. "Every single rally is like a death rattle at the high," runs one typical quote.

Born November 12, 1916, in the Bronx; died July 18 at home in Pasadena of heart problems; survived by his wife, Mei-Lee Ney, and his stepdaughter, Marcia McMartin.

Chapter 10

More Than Words

ALANA BARANICK

Phoebe, actress Lisa Kudrow's somewhat dim-witted character on the TV sitcom, "Friends," believed that the father she had never met was a good-looking, well-dressed man who loved children and dogs.

Her late mother had given her a picture of her absentee father to keep in her wallet. Phoebe's maternal grandmother had a collection of other photos, showing Dad in a meadow, helping a little boy fly a kite and attending several graduations. He posed with a collie for another portrait.

One problem: The man in the pictures was not Phoebe's father, but a model who appeared in the photos that come with picture frames and wallets found in retail stores.

All the family-friendly photos helped Phoebe form a positive image of the man who had deserted her and her mother. They helped her accept her mother's story, that her dad was a famous tree surgeon who never contacted her because he lived in a hut in Burma where there were no phones.

A photo often can say more than words about an individual or, at least, more than the words that appear in the person's obituary. It can enhance or detract from the person's life story.

These can be snapshots, formal portraits (as long as they don't have a copyright) or file photos from your newspaper's or some other publication's archives. Your photo department can work through the Associated Press or other publications to get permission and sometimes pay to use these images.

When accepting a photo provided by the family, be sure to print on the back of the picture the name of the deceased and a mailing address for returning it. These are treasured pieces of family history — handle them with care.

If the relatives choose to email the photo, thereby avoiding the problem of returning or possibility losing it, instruct them to scan the picture as is. Tell them your photo department will take care of isolating the image of the deceased in a group shot and any enhancing that's needed.

Relatives, obit writers and photo editors may differ on what photo or photos should accompany the obit. Consider all points of view. Ultimately, the selection will be determined by the person designated as top dog.

In most cases I would prefer to run an obituary without a picture if the only one available for a 91-year-old woman shows her at the age of 21. Instead of appreciating what the nonagenarian accomplished in her life, the reader becomes consumed with the question, "Why on earth did her family choose such an old picture?"

However, if an obituary goes heavy on an 80-year-old veteran's heroism during World War II, a photo of him as a young soldier in uniform can draw the reader's attention. The same principle can apply for a 70-year-old woman who was a fashion model in her youth. Showing her as she appeared on the cover of Vogue magazine 50 years ago would make sense.

Environmental photos — showing the person at a specific event or location, engaged in an activity or with other people — can be wonderful. And they allow the layout editor or page designer more options for presenting the obit.

Show the recently deceased philanthropist at the groundbreaking for the hospital wing she financed, the dearly departed mayor in front of city hall or the late yacht club commodore sailing his boat.

For readers who couldn't visualize the bubble-making toys that William J. Cajka Jr. had invented, we chose a picture of him showing off one of his creations and the countless bubbles it produced to go with his obituary. The photo had been taken by Plain Dealer photographer David Petkiewicz for a story that ran in our paper a year before Cajka's death.

Cajka was dressed casually with his mostly unbuttoned, short-sleeved plaid shirt revealing the top of a clean white T-shirt. The visor on the ballcap he was wearing was bent into a half-moon shape that accentuated his boyish grin and the childlike wonder on his face.

Although Cajka, who died of lung cancer at age 50, would never be mistaken for actor Tom Hanks, this photo brought to mind the image of Hanks' character in the movie "Big," a boy who was trapped in the body of a man and worked for a toy company.

Nico Jacobellis' obituary featured a 1950 Plain Dealer file photo in which the former movie theater manager was standing near a movie projector and examining a strip of film. Readers could infer immediately that here's a guy who had something to do with movies a long time ago.

In 1959, Jacobellis was convicted on obscenity charges for showing a French film called "The Lovers" at a local movie theater. The film featured love scenes that are tame by today's standards, but were controversial in America — or at least in Ohio — at that time. Jacobellis' conviction was overturned by the broader-minded Supreme Court in 1964.

When Vincent G. Simonetti died in 1995, we ran two pictures of him with his obit. One was a standard headshot in which he was dressed for a special occasion with a white shirt, bowtie and jacket. The other photo, which had appeared on the cover of Life Magazine during the Korean War and later was included in the "Best of Life" anthology, showed Simonetti as a prisoner of war. It was particularly moving.

For Andy Dunlop, who built cars and headed racing teams for the Indianapolis 500, we ran obituary art that was not actually a photograph, but a replication of a book cover. Dunlop, who devised many innovations that made vehicles move faster and allowed pit crews to make repairs more quickly, was depicted on the cover of "Offenhauser," a 1996 Gordon Eliot White book about race car engines. The lifelike illustration, showing him as a mechanic working on a race car, gave readers an understanding of who Dunlop was without their reading a single word of his story.

Dare Wright wrote and photo-illustrated the classic children's book series, "The Lonely Doll," which featured black-and-white photos of a vintage-1920s Lenci doll named Edith and a couple of teddy bears. The first book, published in 1957, made the New York Times Children's Best Sellers list and became tremendously popular with girls ages 4 to 8.

When Wright died, we ran a headshot of her from the 1960s along with a photo of Edith and her teddy-bear friend, which Wright had taken for one of her books. The result was terrific. I later heard from several women who didn't remember Wright but recognized Edith. Seeing the doll stirred their memories of reading the books as kids and later sharing them with their own daughters.

Sometimes it's appropriate to run a picture of the now-deceased campaign worker at a political rally with her candidate of choice; a freshly dead actor in a scene from a play with a movie star; or a departed high school basketball coach with the millionaire hoops star whom he mentored.

If you choose to run an image of the deceased shown with a celebrity, make sure the caption explains who's who and who's dead.

I write a weekly obit feature called "A Life Story" that usually includes four pictures taken of the deceased at various times of life and engaged in a variety of activities. We've used many photos that are standard family-album fare: wedding or prom photos, formal or candid; baby pictures; family portraits; snapshots from a family vacation.

Others are peculiar to the individual. A woman who raised cocker spaniels floating on an inflatable raft in her swimming pool with one of her dogs stretched across her lap. A dairy farmer shown as a youngster with the steer he took to the county fair. A mounted policeman riding his horse.

"A Life Story," which introduces our readers to some Northeast Ohioans they most likely never got to know, was inspired by "A Colorado Life," a magazine-length obit feature that Jim Sheeler created for the Denver Post.

The Denver Post, May 26, 2002

A Colorado Life

MAGICIAN'S TRICKS WERE TREAT FOR MANY: "PROFESSOR SCHMIDT" FILLED DECADES WITH ESCAPES, ILLUSIONS

BY JIM SHEELER, SPECIAL TO THE DENVER POST

The advertisements shout with vaudevillian verve from yellowed newspapers and posters, in words that still sound like Bob Schmidt.

"LADIES AND GENTLEMEN, BOYS AND GIRLS," they blare, "SEE the 20th CENTURY ALADDIN. A MAN OF MAGIC AND MYSTERY."

In the sepia-tone promotional photos, a dapper man in a tuxedo stands beside a levitating woman. In another photo he lies in a box, chained impossibly tight.

"CAN he ESCAPE? See THIS and MANY OTHER TRICKS."

Inside Schmidt's Denver home, nearly nine decades of magic pours through the living room. The guillotine. The escape-proof box. The black top hat that birthed thousands of rabbits. The wand that so many - ladies and gentlemen, boys and girls - truly believed held a special sort of magic.

As the Schmidt family searched through the boxes of tricks and scrapbooks inside the old magician's house, they remem-

93

bered the acts they marveled at, then found a relic from the 1930s that they had never seen: a sign the size of a card table - the biggest advertisement of them all.

"My brother and I found it and we had the same idea," said his son Kim Schmidt. "At first we thought, 'It this appropriate?' Then we agreed, Dad would love it."

At Bob Schmidt's funeral, his family placed the billboard where they knew it belonged: right next to the coffin.

"CHAINED, SHACKLED AND HANDCUFFED," the sign read, "LOCKED IN A MAILBAG AND SECURELY NAILED AND ROPED INTO THIS BOX, PROFESSOR SCHMIDT EMERGES INSTANTANEOUSLY AND FREE OF ALL HIS BONDS!"

Robert E. Schmidt, a.k.a. "Magician Bob Damon," a.k.a. "Professor Schmidt," a.k.a. "The 20th Century Aladdin," died May 9 of a blood infection. He was 90.

Seeing the world

Inside the traveling carnivals in the early 1900s, little Bobby was known to pop his head into the tents, coaxing the performers to share a few secrets. During the day, he helped his parents sell portrait photographs at exhibitions throughout the country. It wasn't long before the boy had become Professor Schmidt, constantly honing his dexterous hands along with his stage shtick.

In 1930s he earned a drama degree from Northern State Teacher's College in South Dakota, then joined the Civilian Conservation Corps, working on construction projects across the country and entertaining the exhausted men at the end of the day. At the onset on World War II, his booming voice and ambitious tricks earned him a place with the USO.

Before the group left to tour overseas during the war an agent suggested that he not perform with a German surname, so Bob looked through his family tree and found an aunt named Damon. The stage name stuck.

While performing with the USO, he played shows literally all the way to Timbuktu - 93 countries and islands in all. It wasn't until the last one that he met the woman who would accompany him the rest of his life.

A Denver native who played organ with the all-female Joy Cayler band, Livvy Taylor was stationed in Japan, homesick, waiting for a letter from Colorado or a transfer back home when she first saw her future husband pull a rabbit out of his hat.

"When we met, I was more interested in M-A-I-L than M-A-L-E," she said, laughing as usual. The couple were soon together onstage and off. They married on his birthday, Jan. 1, and she accompanied him on the organ in variety shows throughout the country.

As television's popularity sucked the life from many live shows in the 1950s, the couple settled in Denver, where Schmidt took a job at Neusteter's department store selling sportswear - a job he would hold on and off until the 1980s. Meanwhile, he couldn't give up the stage.

In the late 1950s the couple joined Pete Smythe's "East Tincup" Old West theme park near Golden, where Schmidt wowed crowds with his Houdini-like escapes and giant props such as his hand-made guillotine, relying on his stage patter as much as the trick itself.

With the "head-chopper" trick, for instance, he would slice an apple in half with the machine, then lock a volunteer's head into place, telling him to hold onto his ears when the blade drops, so he could hoist the dismembered noggin up high once it was lopped off. Schmidt would then begin mumbling to himself, pretending to have no idea what he was doing, and just before the blade dropped, he would hold up the front page of a newspaper, ostensibly from the previous town he played.

"DAMON BEHEADS MAN," the headline screamed; inevitably, so did the volunteer.

In the late 1970s, Schmidt got a small taste of Hollywood, so to speak, landing a role in the low-budget film, "The Legend of Alfred Packer." He played Israel Swann, the first man supposedly devoured by the infamous cannibal.

"I remember turning on the television late one night and thinking, 'I know that guy - the one being eaten,'" remembered his son Rick. "Hey, that's Dad!"

After retiring from Neusteter's, he returned to magic full-time, performing with a traveling variety group and at hundreds of birthday parties for children, where he mesmerized the kids without talking down to them - allowing them to think they had the trick figured out, then blowing their minds.

"It's hard work, and it's a dedication thing. Plus, you really have to be a ham," said his son, Rick. "And Dad was a pure, dyed-in-the-wool ham. A true showman."

'Magic was right medicine'

As they aged, the Schmidts continued to perform for people who truly needed a good escape: developmentally disabled children at Larandon Hall, elderly people at nursing homes, patients at Craig Hospital — along with dozens more.

"Your magic was the right medicine," wrote a nurse from Mercy Medical Center, after one of his many shows.

Even into his late 80s he continued to work at birthday parties and at the Renaissance Festival, where, as an aged, gray-bearded magician walking around the grounds performing sleight-of-hand tricks, many people truly believed he was Merlin.

Though he never officially gave up magic — and was recently honored by the Mile High Magician's Society — the number of shows diminished until he could barely stand. Still, there was one trick he never forgot.

"At the beginning of every show, he would take out an alarm clock and put a satin handkerchief over it, and he would say, 'I only have a certain amount of time to do this for you,'" remembered his son Rick.

Throughout the whole show, the clock would sit onstage, ticking away. Few spectators would notice it until the last trick.

"At the end of the show, the clock would ring, and he would walk over to it and say, 'Boy, doesn't time disappear,'" his son said.

"He would take the handkerchief off, and the clock was gone."

Chapter 11

It's a Wonderful Life

Halfway through the interview, both of us suddenly realized where I was: at his desk, sitting in front of his typewriter. In his chair.

"No, stay there," the old woman said as I moved to get up.

I'll never forget the feel of that man's room as his wife reached for the tissues, just before we shared the afternoon poring through his bookcase, sipping hot tea, in the place where he found his words.

It was while sitting there at the typewriter of a dead journalist that I realized I felt…comfortable.

"Stay," his widow said. "He would have liked you to sit there."

If journalism is a subsidized education, obituary writing is the course in philosophy — for both readers and reporters. The key lies in knowing where to look for the lessons of a life, and not just a list of its achievements.

For me, the rewards of those lessons often center on a crucial question. It's never the first question I ask — sometimes it doesn't even need to be asked. The answer, however, should always be there.

What did you learn from (the name of the deceased)? What did you learn from their life?

It's a question that rarely elicits a quick response — which is understandable. Try to answer it yourself — what did you learn from your (wife, husband, mother, father, sister, best friend…). An easier variation on the question is: How would your life be different if you had never met (the deceased)? The answers are always different, and they're rarely concise. Some of those answers are revealed in these excerpts of obituaries I've included below; many more are only hinted at, deep inside the story.

My own answer — what I've learned from writing about all these lives — takes a while to tell. I'll make my way there with a little help from those people I never met. Most of them won't die until the tenth paragraph.

> Every day, the boy could be found at the same place on that big Missouri farm. For hours he would shovel dirt into a bucket and carry it over to the same spot, where he would dump it onto a pile.
>
> As the sun set, the boy would climb the dirt and look out at the prairie. Each day he stood a little bit higher.
>
> As the years passed, some of the kids made fun of him. Adults just shook their heads. The boy continued to dig.
>
> When they asked him why, the boy tried to explain what he had seen during his family's brief trip to Colorado when he was 3 years old. He had seen something he couldn't forget.
>
> Edward Mallory was building a mountain.
>
> "He worked for several years on that mountain of his," said Frances Mallory, speaking from her living room in Wheat Ridge. "He'd dig the dirt and cart it up there. He said he had no doubt that he would build his own mountain. And he got it up pretty high."
>
> "I don't think I've ever known anyone as drawn to the mountains as my husband," she said. "Lots of people like the mountains. But the mountains were his kindred spirits."
>
> Edward Mallory would eventually spend much of his lifetime scouring backcountry trails throughout the state he once dreamed of. He rarely told anyone what he was looking for, but always described in detail what he found.
>
> More than eight decades later, hundreds of people scurry up the dirt and rocks every year, looking for the place that bears his name.
>
> As a boy, he built a mountain. As a man, he went inside.
>
> Edward Carson Mallory died at Lutheran Medical Center on December 17, 1998. He was 85.

That began the first story in a weekly feature called "A Colorado Life," which I started as a freelance writer for the Denver Post. The key to these stories was that they had never been told; I didn't want to write about anyone whose name had ever appeared in the newspaper.

It's a Wonderful Life

The stories — which usually ranged between 20 and 30 column inches — were approached with the same elements as any feature: with a scene, and a story. And, perhaps most importantly, the intentions of breaking as many rules as possible.

The first goal was to avoid the telephone at all costs - often starting in the place where the dead person felt most comfortable. That's where the best interviews begin.

Though I make my initial inquiries on the telephone, I try to do every interview in person. Not only in person, but in the right place.

In the case of a mechanic, it's best to interview his buddies in the garage, where they can reference parts of his life, and theirs. I want to see the dead piano teacher's student sitting in front of her piano as I speak to him, so he can describe how her wrinkled fingers guided his. I'll drive on tractors with the widows of ranchers as they show off the land, and plumb the cardboard boxes of packrats with their children. That's how I ended up in the old journalist's chair, thinking about my own job, and the one ahead.

Because my obituaries are often as much about what remains as much as what's gone — the living as well as the dead — it is often crucial to see the stuff that made up a life, but also the stuff that arrives after that life is gone. As some of these excerpts show, sometimes, that's all you need.

In a place where the air smells like words, Tom Parson finds one of Elaine Peck's final poems. It weighs about ten pounds.

"This is one of the last things she printed," Parson says as he hefts out a block of lead letters set by her hand.

"Lasso some laughter
When troubles confound you
Let love like an aura of
Peace surround you."

These days, someone could type up the poem on a computer and print it out in seconds. For Elaine Peck, it meant choosing the letters individually from a wooden drawer and lining them up properly on the makeshift metal page, set in reverse. From there, the 80 year-old woman would walk to one of the ancient half-ton machines, and begin clacking away.

Inside his workshop in Denver, where he now stores much of her collection of lead letters, pictures and writings, Parson walks over to a century-old Chandler & Price printing press.

He pushes the treadle with his foot and watches the enormous metal plate kiss the paper, just the way his mentor taught him. When he pulls out the paper, the ink is still fresh:

Ephemeral but precious forever
Elaine Jorgensen Peck
1916-2001

By centering on people who've never been written about — people whose life stories have no "news" rush to get into the paper — there's less of a time constraint. And in many of these articles, spending time in their space is the most crucial part of the story. Most of my stories involve a full day of reporting and a full day of writing. That amount of time is usually unheard of for an obituary — but it's hardly uncommon for someone working on a traditional Sunday feature.

By making my stories more like Sunday feature stories — stories about life and death instead of simply about A life — I argued to the editors that they deserved at least as much attention as the stories at the front of the paper. Though management was skeptical at first, the feature's tremendous response — and reader surveys naming the weekly obituary as one of the most popular features in the paper — I was allowed the freedom to push the traditional constraints of the obit formula.

Because of my broader scope with the stories, I also argued that they were still appealing months after a person's death, and shouldn't have an arbitrary limit of when a person was "too dead" to get in the paper. I was given a window of three weeks from the date of death (though sometimes I stretched it to four).

In some cases — especially as the feature became more popular — I received calls before someone died. For the first few, I told them to call me back after the death. Then I realized I had missed the invitation.

So When Nick Papadakis' daughter called, I couldn't miss the chance to meet her father.

PUEBLO - As the lunch crowd fills the place they call The Deli, the only empty seat is the one with the best view.

The vacant chair is positioned near an old bench covered with shag carpeting, under descriptions of sandwiches that carry the names of the people who eat them: The Jimbo, The Don, The Ralph, The Tom (cheese $.10 extra). For the past 25 years, that seat was reserved for a guy named Nick, who never thought to name a sandwich after himself.

"Tell Nick that Bo was in, okay?" a man tells the workers

behind the counter, after seeing the empty chair. Another guy chimes in, "Tell Nick that I said Hi, willya?"

Inside The Deli that Nick and June Papadakis built, construction workers sit with lawyers; cops eat with county secretaries. A 90 year-old man comes in most every day, the same as he has since the place opened. They're the first to admit they know "this old hole in the wall" too well, so it's tough to miss all that emptiness in the corner.

If Nick Papadakis heard a joke at 11:30 a.m., everyone on Main Street knew it by 1 o'clock, the punchline escorted by a deep belly laugh, powered by an unashamedly deep belly. As he sat in the chair with a view of the entire restaurant, he could match each face with a name, and - more often than not - a sandwich. From his perch at the back of the restaurant, he pontificated and gesticulated, his gruff voice bellowing out opinions on sports, politics, and, most importantly, food.

For several weeks, the noontime crowd has known that Nick won't be there; most have heard about the 64-year-old's fight with lung cancer. As they stream into the restaurant on August 2, however, few are prepared for the phone call.

"His kidneys are failing," Nick's daughter, Michele Carpino says after hanging up her cellphone, relaying a message from his hospice nurse: "It's only a matter of hours."

As the extended family closes the restaurant to return to his bedside, Nick's wife of 43 years looks back at his chair.

"I don't know what we're going to do with it when he's gone," June Papadakis says. "There's just an empty space here. There's a hole."

To find the first scene of the story, it often takes quite a bit of reporting before the actual interview — such as inquiries to find out whether the funeral will be worth attending, especially if there is an elaborate memorial service or unusual setting (Elk's Lodge, bowling alley, neighborhood bar). By spending this hour or two of reporting time at the funeral — sometimes with no more than a handshake and introduction to the survivors — the connection can lead to an invitation into places — both physical and emotional — that reporters are rarely invited.

Finding the best place to meet someone for an obituary interview can usually be accomplished with a few quick questions — where did they spend the most time, where did they feel most comfortable — and once there, allowing the survivor to get up and roam through their space, picking up books and flipping to dog-eared pages, sifting through scrapbooks and telling the stories behind the pictures, or holding an old trophy while trying to figure out what it meant so long after big game.

In some cases, with questions such as, "How do you plan on remembering him? Do you plan on visiting any of her favorite places?" it's possible to watch a life unfold again.

Some of the best obituaries occur in present tense.

Bob Engel parks his car in a patch of overgrown weeds near the railroad tracks in Eastern Colorado, at a place where the train no longer stops.

"This is it," he says. "This is where the depot was.

"This is where my mother was born."

He walks along in the weeds and dry wheat and pauses under an old cottonwood tree.

"My grandparents planted these trees," he says. "There's not much left, now."

In the back of his car sits a vase full of roses, cut from his backyard in Denver. Whenever he comes back to Agate, he always brings roses for his mother and his aunt. Today, his aunt will get them all.

He walks out of the weeds and shakes his head.

"The railroad really should take better care of this place," he says.

Agate, population: 70, is one of those towns that people describe as "blink and you'll miss it."

Lois A. Engel loved living in the blink.

As Lois Engel's story continues, we learn about a lost life and a lost town. We tour what's left of it with the people who remember what's no longer there.

During that interview, while digging through his mother's old home — and sharing plates of heirloom tomatoes — Mr. Engle found an old letter written when his mother was 9 years old, in 1931, after she had lost a tooth.

"Dear fairies," the letter begins, "I don't suppose you will bring me anything because all the banks went busted, but bring me a dime if you can. Well, I will close with love, Lois D."

Often, the key to unlocking a life comes in the deceased's own words. I always ask to look through letters, saved e-mails, journal entries — anything that I can quote from the dead person's own pen. In many cases, they'll lead you right to the life story; in the best cases, they'll write the stories for you.

It's a Wonderful Life

Shortly after I began "A Colorado Life," I received an e-mail late one night from a woman who, after years of reading the obituaries that traditionally made it to the news pages, wondered if there was space for her son.

"My son wasn't an athlete, he wasn't killed violently," she wrote. "He was just a regular teenage boy who died in my arms the other night." After a few hours at her home, I realized he had already written the story for me.

At the top of the page, the title is scrawled in the impulsive script of a 14 year-old boy: "Code of Morals." Near the bottom of the page is a signature, "Daniel Seltzer 5-24-98."

Between them, words to live by, and to leave behind.

1. All moral decisions should be weighed by determining if the overall benefits outweigh the costs.

"I found the list in his drawer, while I was going through his room," said Fern Seltzer, as she looked over the words scribbled on notebook paper in her son Daniel's handwriting.

"Occasionally he would refer to these," she said. "He would recite them from memory. He put a lot of effort into them."

2. Religion only brings about hatred, war, and conflict; never peace or

unity.

His "Code of Morals" includes the words of great thinkers and some of his own, adopted and narrowed down to 10 guidelines. The list was not completed for a class. Nobody told him to write it.

As with most of Daniel Seltzer's passions, it was sparked by a searing quest for knowledge - a search that would pile a lifetime of learning into a body that was never old enough to drive a car.

Daniel Seltzer died suddenly and unexpectedly at home Feb. 13, of complications from a previously undetected heart condition. He was 15.

3. Never allow fear to run one's life...

Daniel's obituary is punctuated by his code of morals, building to the end, when he provides his own last words. To me, the endings are just as important, if not more than, the beginnings. After all, these are obituaries — stories essentially based on the end.

Because of that, I've always been against ending the obituary with a list of survivors. After all, these stories are written for the reader, not the family and friends. One solution to this is to place all the information on survivors in a fact box somewhere else on the page. That way the ending is reserved for the end.

I never leave an interview without an idea for that ending; I'll stay for hours until I have at least an idea of where the life will finish. One of my favorites happens to be about one of the crustiest characters I ever (never) encountered…

…When he finally went to the hospital, Charley was known to give endless grief to the doctors and nurses — he would take out his pocketknife and started messing with the oxygen mask, trying to improve it. For a while, they brought him his 5 o'clock "happy hour" beer he drank most of his life. And if anyone didn't like it he'd tell them where they could go (when people asked him what the "C.B." stood for in "C. B. Lovell," he told them, "constant bitch").

When asked what a compliment from him sounded like, the family members are quiet. That's their answer.

"He didn't say it, you just…knew (he was proud)," Jim says. "I'd go to the same places that he went, and if he wasn't there his friends would say, 'Boy your dad's been talking you up a storm.' That's how you knew."

"He wasn't a real touchy-feely type of person," says his daughter Phyllis. "But you knew it if he didn't like you. If he thought you were full of s—, he'd tell you to your face."

After his death, the family gathered in a hospice room at the hospital to share a few somber moments, and more than a few smiles. "No bulls—," he had told them.

"When he did pass on, we spent the day in the room, sitting on the bed, telling stories, saying that we should have a beer at five o'clock," Phyllis says. "We were sitting there and my husband came in and after a while he said, 'You know, that's probably the longest I've ever been in the room where he wasn't cussing at me.'"

Inside the Lovell house, the family laughs again.

"It was difficult in the beginning," agrees daughter-in-law Cheryl Lovell. "But when you got to know him, you learned to appreciate him."

Later, as Jim Lovell walks up his driveway a few blocks away, he pauses at his father's gold 1971 El Camino in the driveway.

"He wanted to ride in it again before he died," Jim says of the car - one of dozens that he and his father worked on much of their life. "He will ride it again when we go scatter the ashes on the way to Estes Park. He wants them scattered from the El Camino."

As he walks past the car, Jim Lovell thinks back to the last conversation with his father, as he lay dying. It was Valentine's Day in Loveland, and his father hugged him from his hospital bed, struggling to whisper his last instructions:

"'Take care of s——.'"

Another ending is just poignant, if not as blunt.

This last excerpt comes at the end of the life of a hospice nurse whose words I still re-read, and whose family continues to amaze me.

Of all the front page news stories I've ever written, I can only think of a few that I would ever bother to look at again. The best obituaries — like the lives — are the ones that still make us think, the ones that still teach.

As usual, someone else said it better than I ever could.

"Dying is never easy," Carolyn Jaffe wrote. "Suffering and grief are always part of dying. But closeness and warmth can be there, too. If I've done my job well, I feel the warmth and the closeness. I share the laughter and love. I know I've made the time better. I've changed the dying from something that's feared, something that's the enemy, to a natural part of life - maybe even a friend. The families tell me this, and I know it without their saying a word. This is powerful; it is beautiful."

Carolyn Jaffe didn't die at home. Still, co-workers say, hers was a hospice death.

In September a heart problem sent her to the hospital and doctors scheduled surgery, then decided that her weakened body couldn't take the stress. Before she could be sent home, she had another heart attack, and was given only hours to live.

Her daughter Mindy was already on a plane from Hawaii, where she serves as a state representative. Her son Evan was on his way from New Jersey, where he is a Rabbi. Carolyn allowed doctors to use a respirator to keep her alive for the few hours it took for her children to arrive. As she raced to the hospital, Mindy thought back to all her mother had taught, and wondered about what she was about to see.

"I didn't know how I would react. I've never been to a funeral. I've never seen a dead person before," Mindy said.

"But we weren't afraid. I somehow knew it was nothing to fear. We were real prepared because we had talked about it for 30 years."

Once the family finally made it to her hospital room, Carolyn scribbled on a note that it was time for her to go. When the tube was removed, her body would last about 40 minutes.

As the little white haired lady drifted away, her husband and children gathered around and held her hands. Her daughter bent down to her, as close as a person can get.

"As she was taking her last breaths, I got up next to her and breathed in the air as she breathed it out," Mindy said. "She gave me my first breath, and I was taking in her last.

"For me, it was a passing of the torch. I felt very comfortable, right there, breathing in my mother's last breaths. It seemed like the most natural thing in the world.

"It was a lovely goodbye."

So, back to the answer to that most difficult of questions, the one that I've asked hundreds of people, and struggled for hours over countless stories trying to answer. What did I learn from all of these dead people I've never met?

They taught me how to live.

MONTE VISTA MAN MADE AN ART OF LIVING ON A LIMB

JIM SHEELER, ROCKY MOUNTAIN NEWS

Atop his sprawling treehouse among a dozen cottonwoods, the man with the blurry face looked through thick glasses, and watched the world through the leaves.

On his perch 20 feet above the ground, Doug Donnelly stood on warped wood that nobody had wanted. The 41-year-old climbed on legs that doctors told him would never work. He designed the treehouse with a mind that was once called useless.

But for those people willing to venture up into the trees, Mr. Donnelly held out his hand and gave a low chuckle. He then pointed to the ladders that led into his branches and showed them where to hold on.

"Our lives - and his world - were totally different," said his sister, Colleen Donnelly Dean. "But thank God for his world. It's an amazing place."

Douglas Patrick Donnelly died Jan. 17 in Monte Vista, after having a heart attack in his sleep, his family said. He was 41.

When he was born, the infant's face looked out of focus, his eyes crossed, and his features seemed smoothed away. Doctors would later say he had some characteristics of Down syndrome, but their initial diagnosis said only "he would be severely mentally retarded," and suggested the best home was an institution. According to his mother, that was never an option.

"We weren't sure what kind of life he was going to have," said Phyllis Donnelly. "It wasn't long before we knew it was going to be a good one."

Due to nerve damage, young Doug couldn't really smile, his mother said, but anyone could tell when he was trying, because he twitched from cheeks to forehead.

"His smile," his mother said, "was all over his face."

Despite the doctors' initial observations, the family soon realized that the little boy was far more intelligent than most people thought. He attended public schools, taking a combination of special education and regular classes.

Along with school came inevitable teasing, but he found defenders in close friends from his tight, rural neighborhood east of Boulder. Eventually, he figured out how to fight back on his own.

"Even if you did tease him, it wasn't long before he would be your friend," said Chris Clyncke, a longtime neighbor and lifelong pal. "If you laughed at him, he'd just laugh back at you. Because he knew better. And then he was teasing you. It was amazing - you'd think you were getting Doug, and instead Doug would get you."

It wasn't long before he was among the most popular kids in school. In eighth grade, he was elected class president of Nevin Platt Junior High, after promising to bring more junk food into the lunchroom (once administrators told him his platform was impossible to implement, he respectfully resigned).

Then in 1982, he accomplished another goal that some said was unattainable: He walked across the stage at Boulder High School, diploma in hand. When he turned around, he was met with a standing ovation.

After graduation, Mr. Donnelly took a job on an assembly line at a company that made medical devices; when that company moved overseas, he took a similar job, and worked full time until recently.

Still, few friends or co-workers knew of the problems they couldn't see: a malformed spine that resulted in back problems, throbbing in his legs and other periodic medical problems.

The face that wouldn't allow him to smile properly, his mother said, also kept him from crying.

"He was in pain every day of his life," Phyllis Donnelly said. "But very few people knew it."

Mr. Donnelly began each day before the sun, in front of the newspaper, then stacks of magazines - especially Scientific American and Discover - poring over each article, circling key phrases, rearranging words and sentences, responding to articles in his own block letters.

"Who was the first Hominid?" Posed a headline in a recent issue of Discover.

"My ex-boss was the first subhuman," Doug replied.

"Why do we walk upright?"

"To get a better view," he wrote.

He often spoke in silly antonyms constructed to make people giggle, delivered in his deadpan, Eeyore-like drone: Safeway was "Dangerouspath." City Market was "Town Market," and Wal-Mart was "Mal-Wart."

"He makes you pause and stop to appreciate those things that you never see," said Brian Cabral, assistant head coach of football at the University of Colorado, who lived with the Donnellys while attending CU, and shared the basement with Doug.

"So many little things," Cabral said. "Simple things."

When his family moved to Monte Vista in 2002, it wasn't long before Mr. Donnelly saw the forest, the trees and the opportunity. Soon, he was hitching rides on trucks to the lumber store, asking if they had any wood they didn't need. With the help of his extended family he quickly built a place of his own, where he read his magazines and science-fiction books, watched the world, and fell asleep to the rush of the nearby Rio Grande.

At the funeral in Boulder on Friday, his nephew Tyler Dean read from one of his uncle's most prized possessions, a book that Mr. Donnelly enjoyed so much he bought two copies: Treehouses, the Art and Craft of Living out on a Limb.

Inside a church packed with nearly 300 mourners, Tyler

read a poem from a well-worn copy of the book - one that had
spent hours with Mr. Donnelly, up in the branches:

Treehouses

"They inspire dreams
They represent freedom
from adults or adulthood
from duties and responsibilities
from an earthbound perspective.
If we can't fly with the birds
at least we can nest with them."

Chapter 12

Let Me Count the Ways

ALANA BARANICK

Jim Sheeler started "A Colorado Life" more than two years before the New York Times ran the first of its "Portraits of Grief" vignettes about victims of the World Trade Center attack of Sept. 11, 2001.

I suspect the media hype and overwhelmingly positive reader response to the Times' poignant series played a role in the resurgence of personality-profile obituaries in newspapers across the country, even though the brief "Portraits" were severely lacking in details traditionally expected in obituaries. The short pieces gave us a feel for what kind of person the deceased was, but they didn't tell us where the victims came from, who their relatives were or what they accomplished in life before dying so tragically.

But that's okay. The beauty of obituaries is that there is no single way to do them.

A reporter can fashion a memoir from his personal recollections, if the decedent was a friend or someone he covered for years. In certain cases, the writer can use the story of a person's life to shine a spotlight on social issues, such as domestic violence, drug addiction or the homeless.

The obits can use the events in the dearly departed's life to teach readers about the Civil Rights Movement, the Second Vatican Council, the Apollo space program and the development of cellophane.

We obit writers have to get the facts right, adhere to our respective newspapers' policies and work within the limitations set by individual editors. Other than that, we can be creative in our presentation of a person's last writes, beginning with the lead paragraph.

A basic obit might begin with a simple death sentence.

"Lucille Perk, who will always be remembered as the woman who declined a presidential invitation to the White House because it was her bowling night, died of congestive heart failure Saturday at St. Michael Hospital."

Or an announcement of funeral arrangements.

"Services for Otto C. Niederer Sr., an engineer with the Bell Laboratories team that installed the first transatlantic telephone cables, will be at 10 a.m. today at Immaculate Conception Catholic Church, 2846 Hubbard Road, Madison."

You could peg it on some other memorial event.

"A musical jam session in memory of Mike Ruth, who played trumpet with the touring Glenn Miller and Tommy Dorsey orchestras in the 1980s, will begin at 5 p.m. Sunday at Bolich Middle School, 2630 13th St., Cuyahoga Falls."

Pegging the obit on a time hook, like the date of death, funeral or memorial event, is natural. Otherwise it's not news.

Some newspapers may run obits as much as two months after the death. For others, the news window may be narrower. The papers may require the obituary to be printed within a few days of the death or no later than the day of the funeral.

In some cases, the obit writer can use events at the funeral to start the profile of the deceased's life.

"Incense filled the sanctuary of St. Nicholas Croatian Byzantine Catholic Church as parishioners offered prayers for the late Ella Kekic, a former tavern owner who had been their matriarch.

"After the priest gave the service-ending blessing, 'We went into the basement and had a beer,' said Jodi Schaef, one of Kekic's 15 grandchildren.

"Kekic, who died Jan. 29 at 102, was an infant in 1901 when her saloon-keeping parents and 13 other Croatian families in the St. Clair Avenue neighborhood conceived a plan for St. Nick's, a church that felt like home."

Postfuneral events, such as the establishment of a memorial scholarship, dedication of a library in the decedent's name or coverage of mourner reaction can widen the window of obit opportunities.

"At their bimonthly luncheon tomorrow, Greater Cleveland Regional Transit Authority retirees will remember two of their own, Nick A. Mongulo and Kenneth L. Fiedler. The two men were believed to have been the last of the former Cleveland Railway System's double-decker bus drivers."

111

I could have opted to wait a day and started that obit with what the transit authority retirees said about their deceased co-workers at the luncheon.

Because the retirees were mourning two of their peers, who died within a day of one another, I was able to combine the two bus drivers' obituaries into one story, which I call a "double obit." But I wouldn't have done it if the two men hadn't been good friends and their families hadn't been agreeable to it.

I have written double obits for other pairs — a parent and child, a pair of siblings, two city councilmen — but most have been for married couples whose deaths happen within a short time of one another.

Even "Six Feet Under," the HBO series about a family that runs a funeral home, has addressed the two-in-a-row death syndrome.

In the opening scene of each "Six Feet" episode, somebody dies, usually as the result of a freak accident or violence. Fictional character Hattie Jones defied the series norm by dying in her sleep.

The Jones episode begins with Hattie's husband waking up in the morning and egging her on to get up and fix his breakfast. When she doesn't stir, he squeezes her shoulder and calls her name a few times. Then reality hits him. She ain't never getting up.

For the rest of the program, Mr. Jones spends most of his time in the funeral home, sitting in a chair next to his wife's casket, holding her hand and tapping into the reservoir of wisdom he acquired over 56 years of marriage to dispense advice about love, marriage and sex to anyone within earshot.

At the end of the episode, Mr. Jones is at his post next to his wife's coffin, apparently asleep. Nate Fisher, the funeral director, says, "Mr. Jones, it's time to go home." He calls the old man's name a couple of times, before he realizes that Mr. Jones, like his wife, ain't never getting up.

Sometimes it happens like that with old married couples. One dies and, a short time later the other follows. Whether combined or written separately, these husband-and-wife stories can be incredibly touching.

Lou Roch's obit ran a few days after that of his wife of 64 years, Evelyn.

In his obit, I explained that the 89-year-old man lived alone for seven years while his wife stayed at a nursing home. His son answered Roch's telephone when word came that Evelyn had died.

"He kept looking at me like a little puppy dog," the son said. "He asked, 'How is she?'"

Upon hearing that his wife was gone, the elder Roch dropped his head in sorrow. During calling hours at the funeral home, "he allowed them to put him in a wheelchair," his son said. "I knew he was saying, 'I'm done.' "

After the funeral, Roch put a rose on his wife's coffin. Then he was wheeled to a car where he was to wait while the rest of the family visited the grave of another relative. The family returned to the car a few minutes later and found Roch dead of a massive heart attack.

When I learn about the deaths of the two people soon enough, I can combine their stories. I explain the timing and circumstances of each of their deaths. I include biographical information for each person.

When listing surviving relatives for a married couple, I say that they are survived by "their" children, grandchildren, etc. Then I add their brothers and sisters separately. "She also is survived by a brother. He has two surviving sisters in Italy."

It's not always appropriate to combine two obits, even when there's an obvious connection. For example, we wouldn't combine the obits for a husband and wife who died on the same day if it was a murder-suicide, although we might run a news story on the event.

AT MY PAPER, POLICE BEAT and general assignment reporters usually do the stories for folks who are murdered, die in traffic accidents or contract fatal contagious diseases that could pose a health risk to the public. Whenever they can, they include biographical and funeral service information.

The news story serves as the obituary. It may focus more on the circumstances of the death, but it also provides families and friends abundant opportunities for positive input.

We give some folks the opportunity to eulogize prominent people before they're dead. Yes, it's a fact: We do prepare obituaries in advance for big-time movers and shakers.

Our editors tend to assign advance obits to beat reporters who have written about these people in life. Business reporters pen advances for corporate leaders. City hall reporters write them for city officials. Religion, entertainment and sports writers take care of obits for their famous folk.

And that's as it should be. The guest-star obit writer already has a vision for what the story should say and needs only to verify facts through research and interviews.

Getting biographical information and setting up an interview with the famous person for the obituary can be tricky. You can start by asking the person's press representative or secretary for an updated bio for your newspaper's files. If the conversation leads to the subject of "obituary," and you feel comfortable about it, seek an interview with your subject.

113

Big-timers who are getting old and recognize their own importance to the community often figure out what you're up to before you ask. Others may be too modest or hold superstitions that preclude such an interview. In those cases do your best to piece things together from your archives.

Most of the time we get a couple of comments from prominent supporting players or competitors of the not-yet-dead ahead of time. Of course, when the time comes for the obit whoever is plugging in the day of death, funeral arrangements, etc., must make sure that the people quoted are still alive.

In the normal course of reporting, the beat reporter can ask, "How has Insert-Name-of-Community-Leader-Here shaped our city, our laws, our world? What has been her most significant contribution to the community? What do you admire about him?"

The same type of questions can and should be asked when obit showtime finally arrives. You have to steer people away from giving useless quotes like, "He was a wonderful person who will sorely be missed by all." Get the person you're interviewing to explain what made the deceased so wonderful and why he will be missed, sorely or otherwise.

When the person is such a big deal that we pen the obit in advance, the story will probably wind up on the front page or a section front. It's best to get the fact of the person's death in the first two sentences. After all, the death is the reason for the story.

"Former Cleveland Mayor Ralph J. Perk, 85, a Depression-era ice peddler who rose to the city's highest office with the support of blue-collar, ethnic voters, died of complications from prostate cancer early yesterday morning in the Cleveland Clinic Hospice unit of the Corinthian Skilled Nursing Center in Westlake."

I MUCH PREFER TO START AN OBIT, as I would a personality profile, with a compelling lead that makes the reader want to know more about the deceased, particularly if the decedent is not famous. I kill off the departed after I've finished my thought.

"Helen Lubitsky was hard to miss, riding her 1949 J.C. Higgins bicycle through downtown Elyria, wearing her hair and makeup in the style of the 1940s and toting a bag of empty aluminum cans along with a half-filled can of cat food.

"She supplemented her Social Security checks by rummaging through trash bins, often in the early morning just after the bars closed, in search of aluminum cans, which she redeemed for cash at recycling centers. Bouncers, merchants and police looked out for her safety.

"A large portion of her income went toward feeding cats — strays and domestic pets who, like her, had homes, but preferred wandering about the city streets.

"Miss Lubitsky, 75, a lifelong Elyria resident, died of complications from cancer Monday at the Oak Hills Nursing Home in Lorain."

Some papers will let you write the bio and wait until the end of the story to say that the person has died. The theory is that if it's running on the obituary page, the reader should know that the person is dead.

If there's no guarantee that the obit will be printed on the designated pages of death, the story should begin with the details of death. You wouldn't want to start reading a nice story on the business page about someone you know only to learn at the end of the piece that your friend has died.

Some editors insist that the death sentence for every obituary be placed high in the story, regardless of the printed location of the obit. In those cases, you can accomplish your mandate without making the lead dull or cumbersome by inserting the phrase "who died on such-and-such a day."

"Gilbert V. Batman, who died Thursday at age 87, helped pump up American Red Cross blood donations in the 1960s by dressing up like his comic-book namesake.

"Life magazine ran a photo of the former Cleveland policeman, wearing a Batman costume and having his blood drawn by a blood-bank volunteer in 1966, when the 'Batman' television series was popular.

"Gil Batman became accustomed to pranksters calling his home in Brook Park and asking to speak with Batman. He often went along with the joke, pretending to be the Caped Crusader and warning those who challenged him that his electronic bat-locator was homing in on the caller's location."

YOU CAN GAIN INSPIRATION and pick up new ways of saying the same old thing by reading obituaries written by reporters who don't usually pen obits and life stories printed in other publications.

Jim Sheeler's "A Colorado Life" in the Denver Post led to my being able to write "A Life Story" features for the Plain Dealer. My stories are longer than our usual length for obits, but much shorter than Jim's stories. We run an information box and extra photos under which we cram all kinds of nifty information and quotes that we couldn't fit in the story.

It took 18 months for me to persuade my bosses to let me do the weekly Sheeler-inspired feature. I'm still trying to convince them to start running photo-caption obits a la Stephen Miller.

Don't be afraid to think outside the pine box when writing obits. Try something different. You truly can have fun writing about the dead.

PEGGY LEE COLE,
WAS RODEO STAR IN 1930S

By Alana Baranick, Plain Dealer Reporter

Cleveland — Peggy Lee Cole refused to be roped in by the taunts of men who beefed about women rodeo performers.

Their barbs spurred the Wellington native to take the bull by the horns and master several events on the Midwest rodeo circuit in the 1930s and 1940s. The tall, slender redhead became an expert in women's barrel racing, bareback riding and Brahmanbull riding.

Rodeo advertisements billed "Peggy Lee" as a woman who could break any four-legged animal. Rodeo-goers were encouraged to test the claim with feisty animals. Mrs. Cole broke donkeys, horses, goats, hogs, bulls and any other animal that could hold her weight.

She also trained horses for exhibition and competition. Her most famous trainee was Dale Evans' horse, Buttermilk.

Mrs. Cole, 78, of Cleveland, died March 11 at the Pearlview Skilled Nursing Center in Brunswick. She had Parkinson's disease.

Her spunky nature became evident during her childhood in Wellington. She hated her given name - Thirza Maude Witbeck - and refused to answer to it after starting school in Wellington. Friends dubbed her "Peggy," and teachers called her "Miss Witbeck."

She left home at age 17 to join the rodeo.

Around 1950, Mrs. Cole quit the rodeo and moved to Lambertville, Mich., where she raised her two sons. There she boarded and trained horses for competition in English riding, western riding and jumping.

In later years, she trained thoroughbreds for racing.

Her knack with animals was not limited to horses. In the early 1970s, she trained a pet turkey to help dogs that herded horses.

She once took in a pair of orphaned raccoons that became her housepets.

In 1978, Mrs. Cole moved to Willis, Texas, where she lived for seven years. She returned to Northeast Ohio in 1985 to stay with her daughter-in-law, Susan Hedges, on Cleveland's West

116

Side.

Mrs. Cole outlived both of her sons. Arlo Hedges, who was Susan's husband, died in 1982. Robert Hedges died in 1993.

Survivors include her granddaughters, Theresa Hedges-Wydick of Columbus, Tracy Hedges-Kline of Cleveland Heights and Rachel Hedges of Toledo; and two great-grandsons.

Memorial services will be the morning of April 2 at Pearlview Nursing Center, 4426 Homestead Dr., Brunswick 44212, at a time to be announced.

Memorial contributions may be made to the Activities Department at the nursing center or to the Memorial Fund of First United Methodist Church, P.O. Box 315, Willis, Texas 77378.

The Coreno Funeral Home of Cleveland is handling arrangements.

Chapter 13

Fast Eddie Watkins and the Disgraceful Dead

ALANA BARANICK

Fast Eddie Watkins freely admitted his dirty deeds and loved spinning yarns around them, often altering the details depending on the listener. So when the colorful bank robber died, I had no qualms about including his criminal record, or at least a portion of it, in his obituary.

But it's not always that easy to write obituaries for the less than saintly.

In the "Obituaries" episode of HBO's "Oz," actor Harold Perrineau says:

"You gotta pity the guy who's had one thing go wrong in his whole life. I mean, other than that one thing . . . he led a good, average life. But some incident or other, some bad decision or bad behavior, which maybe gained him a moment of notoriety, that'll be the headline in his obit when he dies. You know, like Charles van Doren, quiz show scandal. No matter what else he's done, that's how he'll be remembered. Forever and ever."

People don't have to be notorious to be remembered for one act, one split-second decision, one personal judgment that brought them into the national spotlight and made them fodder for late-night talk-show comedians.

You can probably think of famous people whose obits were or will be shaded by a scandal or bad decision, including a couple of U.S. presidents, some professional athletes and a few show business veterans.

I once wrote an obit for a man who used his multiple positions as a real estate agent, elected public official and state-level executive with a major religious denomination to rehabilitate housing for low-income residents in a financially depressed, crime-ridden area of his city. He did a lot to help his constituents, but somewhere along the way he screwed up and broke the law. It was all over the papers back then.

If he hadn't been such a prominent public figure, I would have winked and simply not written his obit when he died 30 years later. I mentioned his good deeds in his obituary. Yet I could not omit his well-publicized bad one. I felt it was too big and too much of a betrayal of the public trust.

I tried to be fair and balanced. Halfway through his obit, I inserted that he was found guilty of embezzling more than $30,000 in taxpayers' money from a public fund which he controlled. I added that he served six months behind bars to illustrate that his crime was bad enough to merit jail time, but only bad enough to require six months of his life.

You'd have thought I crucified him. I got complaints from his family, his constituents and even readers who had never heard of him.

Their objections fell into three categories. The first, and the one that I've grown to expect, stems from the perception that an obituary is a tribute to the deceased, and not a mini-biography or news story. Readers with this preconceived notion can't understand why anything negative would be included in anyone's obituary. These are the type of folks who think it was wrong to mention the Watergate scandal in President Richard M. Nixon's obituary.

The second area of complaint was voiced by people who knew the late public official and also knew of his indiscretion. Most of them used the same words. "It's not like he killed anyone." They felt he took money that the state government would have misspent anyway. They may have been right, but they didn't consider that ultimately they and their neighborhood friends were the ones he robbed.

The third complaint took me by surprise. Because the public official was a black man, I was accused of racism. A couple of callers suggested that I wouldn't have mentioned his legal problems if he had been white. How wrong they were! I've handled obituaries for other public figures with lighter skin tones and known illegal, immoral or unethical behavior in similar fashion, sometimes even more in-depth.

I didn't flinch in telling it like it was when I penned the obit for a former sheriff who happened to be white. During his eight years as sheriff, he battled the news media, county commissioners and other county and city officials as fervently as he fought crime.

His uninhibited bursts of colorful language were a delight to reporters. In one televised press conference, he compared himself to legendary law enforcers Wyatt Earp and Eliot Ness.

Deputies and government officials frequently described him as paranoid. He seemed to be convinced, according to one newspaper report, that the entire structure of county government, combined with segments of the city's news media, had decided to limit his authority and even drive him from office.

After county commissioners questioned him about his department's overspending $24,000 in less than two months, he called the commissioners "back alley politicians who stifle progress on fighting crime."

In his final year in office, the sheriff was under fire because of a state audit that charged he owed the county more than $92,000 that was unaccounted or illegally spent. In addition, key members of his staff were convicted of crimes in office.

I have passed on writing obits for numerous less prominent individuals with varying skin hues. Like the building inspector for a small Cleveland suburb who reportedly took bribes from developers. The street department supervisor who went to prison for 15 years for stealing thousands of gallons of his department's gasoline and reselling it at his own gas station. And the lawyer who was disbarred for stealing money from the bank account of an elderly client.

I once received written information from a woman who wanted me to write an obituary for her brother, who was in his mid-40s when he died in another town. She said her brother ran a successful business in Cleveland until he was in his late 30s. I wondered what kind of business he ran, why he gave it up, what he'd been doing during the last six years of his life and why he died in a town which is the site of a state penitentiary.

A search of our archives revealed the answers to all my questions. The woman's brother closed up his retail shop and moved because he was sent to prison. For killing his mother!

I decided not to write his obituary. He had not been a prominent businessman, public figure or career criminal. And the news coverage of the murder was relatively brief. When I told his sister that we wouldn't be writing his obit because of his unfortunate situation, she said, "You mean you couldn't write his obituary without mentioning that?"

On the other hand, the daughter of another man relished the notion of an obituary that portrayed her father as a tavern owner and bookie, akin to the characters from the musical, "Guys 'n Dolls." Her dad ran a bar where judges, businessmen and professional sports figures rubbed elbows and placed bets with gamblers and racketeers. Because his previous criminal record as a bookie barred him from holding an interest in a liquor permit, he could not put his name on the title of the saloon. So he put its ownership in the name of a trusted relative, while he acted as the

Fast Eddie Watkins and the Disgraceful Dead

tavern manager.

With his daughter's encouragement, I included all of that information plus subsequent charges of prostitution and lewd behavior that were made against the establishment. I explained that, in the eyes of the law, the relative, whose name appeared on the deed to the bar, bore the responsibility for things that went on at the bar.

After the story was printed, I heard from the dead man's unhappy son, who did not share his sister's point-of-view.

WHEN TO DECLARE THE DECEASED "DISGRACEFUL" is rarely clear. Here are some examples of people whom some might consider shameful, unethical, immoral or downright evil. You be the judge. The lawyer who defends pedophiles. The minister who has an adulterous affair. The young man who steals his mother's credit card to pay for his girlfriend's breast implants. The girlfriend who persuaded that young man to rob his own mother. The mother who leaves her sleeping toddler in her car on a sweltering summer day while she goes shopping. The mother who leaves her toddler alone at home while she goes to a night club. The public official who gets busted for possession of illegal drugs. The retired autoworker, devoted family man and upstanding community man for 50 years, who late in life is exposed as having been a German concentration camp guard.

No, it's not always easy to write obituaries for the less than saintly.

When I was gathering obituary information for a former appointed city official, some of my older colleagues gave me the impression that this fellow had been a bad apple while serving as the mayor's chief labor adviser 30 years earlier.

The headlines for a series of articles about investigations into the deceased's business and government affairs suggested that was true. Yet nothing in our files indicated that he had been convicted of any crimes. We also ran some stories that showed him to be an advocate for the common man. I interviewed people who thought he was a great American and champion of the underdog.

I didn't want to use quotes from his supporters to paint him as a saint or negative editorials to brand him a sinner, but I needed to get both aspects of his life in his obituary. So I diplomatically wrote: "The impeccably dressed, tough-talking labor leader, was a colorful and controversial figure. Some saw him as a miracle worker who kept the peace between the administration and 39 labor unions representing thousands of municipal employees. Others portrayed him as a shady character with ties to mobsters."

Let's get back to Fast Eddie Watkins. His obit generated more comments from readers than anything else I've written. The complaints far outweighed the few compliments - - mostly from fellow journalists, who thought it was a nifty story, and from people who got to know Watkins in his final years.

Some folks, equating obituaries with tributes, were upset that we wrote about a convict at all. Couldn't we find someone more worthy to write about? Others complained about his obit being on the front page. Many resented my calling him a "folk hero," although that's what he was by definition.

But most of the anger was about the last sentence of the obit, announcing that a memorial service was to be held in the auditorium of the Justice Center. For the record, the memorial gathering was never held. The day on which Watkins' story appeared, someone at the Justice Center put up a sign that said, "A memorial service for Fast Eddie Watkins will NEVER be held here."

County offices and our newsroom were besieged with phone calls from angry taxpayers, demanding to know why a lawbreaker would be honored at an edifice which symbolizes the sanctity of the law. And who was going to pay for this event?

County commissioners were even more interested in knowing who gave permission for the gathering to be held there. Other media reported that the writer of Watkins' obituary (as Bob Newhart would say, "That would be me") was "conveniently" unavailable for comment on the day the obit was printed. (Hey, I couldn't help it. It was my regularly scheduled day off.)

The memorial gathering was not my invention, although it did make a great walk-off for the story. Watkin's friends really did tell me they were planning a memorial gathering at the Justice Center. One of them called before my deadline to confirm the time and place.

I didn't question it. A former corrections department official, who used taped interviews with Watkins as educational tools for law enforcement officers, told me he hoped to have the event at the Justice Center. Another person called me back to say it had been arranged. When the obit hit the fan, and elected county officials started running for cover, everyone disavowed responsibility for the planned gathering.

I admit I was distressed to receive messages from three angry individuals who had been victimized by Watkins at different stages in his career. I hadn't considered the psychological pain he caused. But I still would have written his obit.

COLORFUL BANK ROBBER FAST EDDIE WATKINS DIES

By Alana Baranick, Plain Dealer Reporter

Lakewood — Fast Eddie Watkins, 82, a notorious bank robber whose flamboyant escapades and engaging personality made him a folk hero, died Wednesday at Lakewood Hospital.

During his 43-year career of making unauthorized withdrawals from banks from here to California, Watkins estimated he stole more than $1.5 million from 55 banks. He threatened but never resorted to violence during his heists. He maintained friendly relationships with many of the law enforcement officials who captured him, the judges who sentenced him and the reporters who covered his career.

Watkins spent more than 50 years in county, state and federal prisons, but escaped many times.

"He was a very bright guy who could have been successful at a lot of things," said Brent Larkin, Plain Dealer editorial page director, who spoke with Watkins regularly. "Shortly before he was released from prison in 1995, Eddie promised me there was absolutely 'no chance' he would return to a life of crime. And, for a guy who made a lot of bad choices during his lifetime, it was a promise he kept."

Watkins, a Pittsburgh native, was about 13 when he left his mother's home in South Euclid and hopped a train to California to see his father, a con artist who taught the youngster his trade.

In the late 1930s, the wayward teen was involved in three dozen stickups in Cleveland that brought him his first stint behind bars at the Ohio Reformatory. After that, each time he was paroled or escaped from jail, he went back to robbing banks and fleeing police.

In 1965, he made the FBI's list of 10 most wanted fugitives after robbing five banks in the Cleveland area and another in Columbus. His companions were caught, but Watkins and a go-go dancer, who soon became his wife, eluded police for more than a year, traveling across country, pulling stickups along the way.

The couple gambled away much of the loot in Las Vegas. Then they bought a pet shop in San Francisco across the street from a police station, which Watkins often visited to check out the wanted posters.

They moved to Albuquerque, N.M., and opened a riding academy. While Watkins was there, police stopped him for speeding and arrested him for carrying a concealed weapon. They released him before checking his fingerprints with the FBI. Agents finally caught up with him in Montana.

Back in federal prison in Atlanta, he befriended a medical officer who hired him to manage his cattle ranch in Idaho, when Watkins was paroled again in 1975. He stole his sponsor's car and a gun and began another series of bank robberies.

That October, he gained folk-hero status through a foiled robbery at a Society National Bank branch in a Lorain Avenue shopping center.

Known as "Fast Eddie" because of his ability to get in and out of banks quickly, Watkins was forced to take a stand, when a bank employee tripped a police alarm. Claiming to have a bomb, he took nine hostages and threatened to blow up the bank if his demands weren't met.

During the 21-hour negotiations, Watkins let his hostages know that he did not intend to hurt them. Within the first few hours, he released three of them. As his situation turned bleak, he started crying in front of them, saying he didn't want to go back to prison. He gained their sympathy, telling horrific tales of prison life and lamenting his own bad luck.

After surrendering, Watkins was sent back to the Atlanta prison. In 1980, he escaped again, resumed robbing banks and was captured for the last time after an eight-hour standoff with police on a rural road in Medina County, during which he tossed money from his car and took snapshots of the police.

Watkins was nearly destitute when he came out of the federal prison in Wisconsin in 1995. Only once did he stash away his ill-gotten cash.

He buried about $100,000 near Albuquerque. Years later, he discovered a highway had been built over the site.

He did earn money legitimately, selling his paintings and serving as a consultant on a movie about his life. But in an art-imitates-life finish, the movie was never made because someone embezzled money from the film company.

A memorial gathering will be at 5:30 p.m. Monday in the auditorium of the Justice Center, 1200 Ontario St., Cleveland.

Chapter 14

The Great Pretender

ALANA BARANICK

Assuming the identity of another person is a common theme in movies, plays and novels.

Aliens and androids replace people in science fiction, like "Invasion of the Body Snatchers" and "The Stepford Wives." In the film "The Majestic," Jim Carrey portrays a screenwriter with amnesia, who finds himself in a town where folks believe him to be their missing-in-action hometown hero. Because he's not sure who he really is, he goes along with the townsfolk.

In October 2000, Tom Breckenridge, one of the Plain Dealer's top reporters, wrote about a real-life case of mistaken identity. He learned that an Idaho reporter had contacted Art Modell, former owner of the Cleveland Browns football team, to get a comment on the death of Jim Kanicki, a defensive star for the Browns in the 1960s.

Modell was terribly distressed to hear of Kanicki's death.

Kanicki, still breathing and living in northeast Ohio at the time, wasn't thrilled to hear the news either.

Kanicki wasn't the man who had died. Dead was an Idaho man with a similar name and the physique of a linebacker, five years Kanicki's senior, who apparently told his friends, neighbors and wife of 14 years colorful stories about his gridiron glory days. But those weren't the Idahoan's glory days. They were Kanicki's.

Exactly how this guy, by all reports an upstanding citizen, became known as the former Cleveland Brown in his adopted hometown is unclear. Did he, like Carrey's character in "The Majestic," go along with someone else's misconception of who he was? Or was he trying to impress the strangers, who would eventually become his friends, and the woman who would become his wife?

If the latter is true, he wouldn't have been the first person to do this sort of thing.

I once received obituary information from a funeral director about a man who was described as "a former Ohio Supreme Court judge." I was sure that we would have lots of old newspaper articles about this important public figure in our archives.

Sure enough, his file was chock full of stories about cases he had worked on as a lawyer and about political campaigns for just about every public office for which he was eligible to run. Yet the clips did not show that he ever was elected or appointed to the bench at any level.

I phoned the funeral director to ask why he gave me what appeared to be false information. Or was there some kernel of truth here that he or the family had misinterpreted? I thought perhaps the deceased lawyer had been licensed to represent clients before the state supreme court and that the funeral director had misunderstood the statement. The mortician said, "I only know what the widow told me. I didn't know the guy, and I never heard of him until he died."

I called the Ohio Supreme Court to confirm that this man was not one of theirs. Then I contacted a sitting county judge, whose name had appeared alongside the dead fellow's in some of our old newspaper clips. He knew the late non-judge very well and shed light on the situation.

"You see," the common pleas judge explained, "a few years ago he met this younger woman, whom he wanted to impress."

The would-be state justice ended up marrying that younger woman. His lie didn't die until all of the local newspapers printed his obituary with no mention of Ohio's highest court. I'm guessing his young widow figured things out, but I didn't follow up on that.

Sometimes unpleasant truths about the deceased, even criminal records, have been hidden from the surviving relatives. Family members aren't necessarily trying to re-write history or pull a fast one on the newspaper. They may be clueless, but they generally mean no harm. Those who know that their late loved ones had some shadiness in their lives try to protect their memories or save other surviving relatives from embarrassment.

Many people offer faulty obituary information based on memorable stories their departed loved ones told them. Maybe the tales weren't falsehoods or exaggerations. The surviving relatives may simply have misunderstood the truth about the dearly departed.

Did Grandpa really pitch and play center field for the Detroit Tigers of Major League Baseball? It easily can be verified or refuted. Perhaps he never had an at-bat with the pros, but did play in the Tigers farm system. Or maybe he was a sandlot player with an amateur or semipro team based in Detroit.

Take Uncle Howard's true wartime stories about being held in a German prison camp, stir in a couple of war movies and simmer in the minds of impressionable younger relatives, and you're likely to come up with the idea that Uncle Howard is either the soldier William Holden portrayed in "Stalag 17" or the Steve McQueen character in "The Great Escape."

We avoid saying that someone was "the first" to accomplish a certain feat, unless we can verify it. In some cases, it's obvious that the claim is untrue. But even if we believe it to be true, we can't declare it a certainty without documentation. So we choose our words carefully, saying that a person was "among the first" or "believed to have been the first."

It's always exciting to find out that my obit subjects really were nationally or internationally known in their respective fields.

© The Plain Dealer, June 9, 2003

SCIENCE FICTION'S SUPER FAN; BENEDICT JABLONSKI, 86, KNOWN AS BEN JASON AMONG AFICIONADOS

By Alana Baranick, Plain Dealer Reporter

Benedict Jablonski, mild-mannered clerk-typist for a metropolitan car dealership, morphed into his alter ego, Ben Jason, BNF (Big Name Fan), whenever he entered the realm of SF (Science Fiction).

Jason, who died May 15 at age 86, was 10 years old when Edgar Rice Burroughs' story "Mastermind of Mars," printed in the "Amazing Stories Annual" of July 1927, caught his imagination.

Jason, the son of Polish immigrants, would later:

Have a book dedicated to him by his favorite author.

Design the award known as the Oscar of science fiction.

Chair a world science fiction convention that offered a sneak preview of a television series that took viewers on starship voyages into space, the final frontier.

127

Family entertainment during the Depression often centered on Jason playing the piano while his four brothers joined him in singing such popular tunes as "Glow Worm." They also played pinochle and danced at the Aragon Ballroom.

Jason spent hours reading SF pulp magazines, which gave him a glimpse of a future in which advances in technology would make life more enjoyable.

To connect with other SF bibliophiles, the South High School graduate wrote to pulp magazines and posted notes on bookstore bulletin boards.

"In the late '30s, each city had a small club," said Noreen Falasca Shaw, who met Jason in the 1940s. "People wrote letters to 'Amazing Stories.' They printed their names, addresses, club listings. Then the war came and took care of all that."

Jason's friends believe he kept up with his SF reading while serving in the Army Signal Corps in North Africa and Italy during World War II.

After the war, Jason became a file clerk for Hann Heating and Plumbing and resumed his camaraderie with SF fans, all of whom consider the term "sci-fi" offensive.

"We have an organization called First Fandom for people who were involved in the field starting in the '30s," Shaw said. "We feel we worked a long time to put science fiction on the map. And when it got on the map, people forgot we were there."

One of the markers that the Cleveland group, and Jason in particular, put on the map was Hugo, the trophy that is awarded to creative folks whose work is judged the best in SF.

Jason took a rocket-shaped hood ornament from an Oldsmobile 88, had it retooled and mounted on a base to present to winners at Cleveland's first world SF convention in 1955. He is credited, along with another man, for its design.

In 1965, Jason traveled to a conference in England to garner support for Cleveland's bid to host the 1966 convention. While there, he met his wife, Gladys, whom his friends call "the English woman." Their marriage didn't last long.

Also in 1965, famed SF author, E.E. "Doc" Smith, dedicated his book, "Subspace Explorers," to Jason and gave him the original manuscript.

"Ben read Smith's 'Lensman' series, and wrote a 'Gosh!' fan letter," said fellow SF follower Bill Thailing. "Doc Smith was so overtaken with Ben's letters of 'Gosh! Wow!' praise that a friendship developed."

Jason headed the 1966 convention in Cleveland, at which Gene Roddenberry played the two-hour pilot of his new series, "Star Trek," for SF fans, before the TV show went on the air.

In the early 1980s, after retiring from Williams Ford, where his desk was in a corridor lined with spare parts, Jason opened a tiny SF/comic book store in the Euclid Arcade called Golden Fleece Magazines. He later moved it to an equally cramped storefront on East 55th Street.

"It was more or less a hobby with him," said his only surviving brother, Ernie Jablonski of Brunswick Hills Township. "I'd come in there, and he'd be sleeping behind the counter."

Jason, who became largely disabled due to Parkinson's disease, got a large flat-screen TV, VCR, DVD and computer for his nursing home room last year before his money ran out.

"He was still interested in getting hooked up to the Internet until the last month of his life," said David Brook, his former nursing home roommate. "He was even trying to get a [satellite] dish."

Chapter 15

Warning! Warning! Will Robinson!

ALANA BARANICK

Two elderly men walked into the lobby of the old soldiers nursing home, where their brother was staying, when they noticed the brother's picture on the bulletin board. Under the banner: "In Memoriam."

Their brother was dead.

Naturally, they were shocked. They assumed he had passed away during the last hour, while they were on the road for their weekly visit. They became angry, when they learned he had died earlier that week. Their brother's wife of 12 years hadn't bothered to tell them or his adult children, who lived out-of-state, that he was gone. Or that he was already buried. And without the traditional religious service that his family believed was essential for determining where he would spend eternity.

Adding insult to injury, the widow placed only a short death notice in the local paper, which gave little indication of who the deceased was. She left out his siblings' names, which would have helped identify him to the readers. (In fairness to the widow, I have to figure she didn't want to pay the additional fees for a longer classified ad.)

Presumably at the prompting of her brothers-in-law, she did arrange for a memorial service. But it was to be held in the faraway town in which her husband had lived for only a short time before entering the veterans home. His lifelong friends probably would not go the distance to pay their respects. The brothers ended up scheduling a second memorial service closer to home and placed another death notice with more identifying markers.

Warning! Warning! Will Robinson

I've come across many more life-and-death situations that make me want to cry out the "Warning! Warning!" mantra of the robot from "Lost In Space," but we rarely address these things in print. The obituary is an inappropriate forum. This is the story of a person's life, not an exposé of family problems.

An issue-oriented story would not likely be pursued at my paper without someone filing a lawsuit, thus making it fair game. Even then, it would be difficult to get both sides of the story. Chances are, the editors wouldn't have reporters waste their time on this sort of thing, unless one of the key players was a public figure.

The siblings of the dead veteran could not file a lawsuit against the widow. As his wife, the widow was his recognized next-of-kin. She had the right to do whatever she wanted regarding his final disposition.

The same was true for the widow of a popular firefighter who didn't want to hold public funeral services for her husband and didn't want anything written about him in the newspaper. His adult children by a previous marriage didn't share their father's late-in-life wife's need for privacy. The kids finally were able to get their stepmother to agree to let them arrange (and probably pay for) what they considered a fitting funeral, so his many friends could pay their respects.

However, for some reason the widow did not want her name printed in the paper. As a result, we did not write an obituary for the deserving retired firefighter. It wasn't because the woman had any power to prevent our news department from running an obituary. But if we had written it, we simply could not have ignored her existence. Yet it would have been worse to say that he left a surviving wife, who did not want her name in the newspaper. If the deceased had been a bigtime newsmaker, we probably would have written his obit with a brief mention of his marital status and his widow's unorthodox stance.

In one of the worst stories I've heard, the recently deceased's live-in love interest arranged for his body to be cremated, but did not have the legal right to handle his final disposition. He had adult children surviving him.

From what his kids told me, their father had taken up with this woman after their mother died. He bought a house in another town, filled it with his and his late wife's furniture and other belongings, some of them valuable, and lived there with his new lover. It created a rift between him and his children, who warned that the live-in girlfriend was an opportunist.

The father was only in his 60s. As far as his kids knew, he had not been ill. They kept abreast of his life through mutual friends, who were the ones who informed them that their father had died.

The children learned that their father's lover had his body taken to a funeral home, identified herself as his next-of-kin and ordered his cremation. They called another funeral director, who had taken care of their mother's funeral. He in turn contacted the mortician who was supposed to do the cremation. Arrangements for the funeral ultimately were handled according to the kids' wishes.

In the meantime, their father's girlfriend had hauled away the contents of his house and more-or-less disappeared before they knew it. More upsetting than losing material goods that could be sold was the loss of their parents' personal effects: pictures, birth and marriage certificates and family heirlooms, which had only sentimental value. I should note that I never spoke with the villified woman for her version of what happened. I couldn't find her.

Another story that was never reported was that of a woman who apparently was a few bricks shy of a load mentally. One of her friends told me that when her parents died, they left her their house, so she would always have a home. Then a man came into her life, moved in with her and persuaded her to put her house in his name. When he died, she was kicked out of her lifelong home by her boyfriend's nephew, who inherited the home she'd always known.

It's possible that a good lawyer could have contested the will and convinced a court that the slow-witted woman did not understand what she was doing when she transferred ownership of the house to the boyfriend. But she didn't know that, didn't have anyone to advise her and didn't have the resources to hire a lawyer. She ended up penniless and living in a government-subsidized apartment building.

A few years ago, I wrote an obit for an elderly fellow who did something I consider wonderful. Yet, at the request of his widow, I did not include these specifics in his obituary.

He was around 90 when he married a single mom who was young enough to be his granddaughter. From what I could gather, the man and his first wife, who were childless, had befriended the young woman after she had escaped an extremely abusive relationship.

I'm not clear on whether the young woman and her kids lived with the couple before the old woman died. What is clear is that the kind old gent married the young mom as a formality so that she and her youngsters would have a nice home and could inherit his estate without any legal wranglings upon his death. In return, she took care of him and his home during his final years.

The young widow didn't want that story told, because she feared that the man who had battered her would discover her whereabouts and harm her or her children.

Warning! Warning! Will Robinson

Stay with me now. I'm shifting gears.

I was 40 years old the first time I heard the term "autoerotic asphyxiation." And like most new words that have entered my vocabulary in recent years, I learned it on the death beat.

I received obituary information from a funeral director for a young man who died while home from college for the weekend. The funeral director, who always leveled with me, said the death was accidental.

"Was he in an automobile accident?" I asked.

"No," the mortician said. "He died at home."

"Did he fall down the stairs or what?" I asked.

"Trust me," was the answer. "It was an accident."

I pleaded for more information. After all, how could I write that a man in his early 20s up and died without giving some kind of explanation? The accident part screamed for more details.

The flustered funeral director offered clues, which I'm sure he thought would make it obvious to me what had happened. The young man's body was found in his bedroom closet. Clad in nothing but a necktie. Hanging from the clothes rack. And there was something about a plastic bag, which I still don't understand.

If I hadn't been clueless about the various ways in which people gratify themselves sexually, that would have been enough. But no. Not me. I had to ask, "How in the world could that be an accident?"

Finally, the funeral director said, "I can't tell you more than that, except it's a coroner's case. But trust me, it was an accident."

I was unable to reach the coroner. And the police, who would automatically have been called to the young man's home to investigate his death, would not talk to me about it over the phone. So the night editor sent a young reporter, fresh out of college, to the police station to get the report. She returned, stating matter-of-factly, "Yeah. It was an accident. He hung himself."

I still didn't get it. "How can you accidentally hang yourself in your closet, when you're basically naked?" I asked.

The young woman looked at me incredulously, surprised that I was so ill-informed. She said, "Autoerotic asphyxiation."

My knowledge of language helped me understand immediately that this unfortunate fellow had strangled to death while masturbating, but I still didn't understand the noose. The reporter explained to me that a person can heighten pleasure during sex by cutting off his air supply.

We're supposed to tell our kids that smoking can cause cancer and taking drugs can fry your brain. They see the television warnings, "Don't drink and drive," and "If you are sexually active, use condoms, so you don't get make babies or spread sexually transmitted diseases."

We tell them, "Don't play with guns." "Don't play with matches." And we use the time-honored adage, "If you don't stop it, you'll go blind," as code for, "Don't play with yourself."

But nobody ever told me to warn my kids that masturbation could kill them. After writing that obit (with the words, "died of accidental asphyxiation," not "autoerotic") I went straight home and discussed this with my teenaged sons. I had to. I love them. It's my duty as a mother to protect them from harm.

I wouldn't want to embarrass the already distraught family of the college student who died, and I did not tell the whole story in his obituary. But his death could have offered an opportunity for public instruction on this issue, and, perhaps, have saved some other lives.

I believe that taboo subjects and true stories about bad experiences, even those resulting from inappropriate behavior, should be discussed to help folks avoid falling into the same traps and to help others to turn their lives around. Sometimes the bad elements of a person's life as presented in an obituary can offer experienced-based instruction and hope to others.

© The Plain Dealer, September 6, 1994

BLACK ACTIVIST ALI-BEY DIES; HE LIVED TO 'FULFILL DESIRES OF EQUALITY'

By Alana Baranick, Plain Dealer Reporter

Garfield Heights — Omar Ali-Bey, who turned from a life of drugs and crime to become an outspoken and respected advocate for the black community, died yesterday at Brecksville VA Hospital from an AIDS-related illness. He was 39.

Ali-Bey had spent the last dozen years of his life promoting self-esteem and speaking out against drugs, racism, injustice, gang violence and anything else that threatened the black community, especially in Cleveland's inner city.

At Rep. Louis Stokes' annual 11th Congressional District Caucus Labor Day picnic at Luke Easter Park yesterday, the veteran congressman paid tribute to Ali-Bey, opening a traditional round of political speeches by asking for a moment of silence in Ali-Bey's memory.

George L. Forbes, president of the Cleveland branch of the NAACP, said he sometimes had disagreements with Ali-Bey but nonetheless invited him to speak to a political science class Forbes teaches at Baldwin-Wallace College.

134

Warning! Warning! Will Robinson

"He probably was the most profound speaker, the most exciting that I had," Forbes said. "The kids to this day still speak about it. He was controversial, but he was a man who loved blackness, who loved black people, and he lived his life to fulfill the desires of equality for black people."

Saving the black family had been Ali-Bey's mission in life since he broke free from a world of drug abuse and crime.

He was born Harold Iverson in Cleveland. He dropped out of East Technical High School in the 11th grade.

A year later, he moved to Chicago, where he joined the Blackstone Rangers, a notorious street gang. When Ali-Bey got into serious trouble with the law, a judge gave him the choice of going to jail or joining the Army. He chose the latter in 1973.

While stationed in Killeen, Texas, he first experimented with heroin and began to steal to support his habit. He was convicted of larceny and spent a year at the Army's stockade in Leavenworth, Kan.

After his release from prison and his honorable discharge from the Army, he moved to Atlanta, where he worked in a machine parts factory.

In 1979, Ali-Bey returned to Cleveland, cleaned up his life and enrolled at Cuyahoga Community College to study journalism and business. But his walk on the drug-free path was short-lived.

In 1981, while fleeing police after a robbery downtown, Ali-Bey crashed the van he was driving into a pole and suffered extensive injuries, which left him in a body cast.

As his bruised body began to heal, he realized he was on the track to an early grave. He kicked drugs completely and became a Muslim in 1982.

Armed with a newly found zeal and purpose in life, Ali-Bey re-enrolled at CCC, joined the school's black student union and organized bus rides for events like the African Liberation Day in Washington, D.C.

He earned an associate degree in business management from CCC and a bachelor's degree from Dyke College, where he majored in marketing.

Ali-Bey felt that his life experiences lent a certain credibility to his work steering people away from drugs.

"When they saw I was a good Muslim who turned his life around, people listened to me," Ali-Bey said earlier this year.

Holding to the Muslim edict of self-help and self-esteem,

Ali-Bey called for residents of the King-Kennedy Estates to clean up the buildings and grounds surrounding the housing complex, rather than wait for the city to handle it. When the estimated 200 resident and non-resident volunteers finished clearing the area of trash that Saturday morning in the late 1980s, they decided to use that same spirit of cooperation in an ongoing effort to rid their neighborhood of drugs and crime.

As a result, the Coalition for a Better Life was born, with Ali-Bey as its chairman.

He organized and participated in anti-drug and anti-crime patrols at public housing complexes both in Cleveland and surrounding communities, such as Lorain.

He spearheaded efforts to end youth gang violence, fought for an Afro-centric curriculum in the Cleveland city schools and took the police to task when he felt an injustice had been committed.

Mayor Michael R. White credited Ali-Bey with the idea for a Black on Black Crime Committee in which black men lead the discussion of what to do about rising crime, disease and drugs in the black community.

From the late 1980s through last year, Ali-Bey organized peace summits to promote truces among local gangs and to highlight education and job opportunities for young people.

Last year, he went to Kansas City, Mo., to attend the first national gang summit, where gang members, social workers, Christian preachers and Muslims gathered to open the lines of communication among gangs and establish peace.

In 1989, he traveled to Africa to discuss trade and cultural exchanges. As a merchant who sold fabric and clothing imported from Africa's west coast at various locations around the city, Ali-Bey was familiar with the problems of black entrepreneurs and could see the advantages these trade talks could produce.

His line of work also afforded him more time for his community activism, for which he received numerous honors. He won the first Wings of Hope Award in 1990 from the local chapter of the Southern Christian Leadership Conference for his anti-drug activism. In October, the Black Elected Democrats of Cleveland, Ohio, presented Ali-Bey with its community service award for his extraordinary work to help curb drug abuse and gang violence. In January, he was honored by the Outstanding Leadership Awards committee for his sacrifices to the community.

Warning! Warning! Will Robinson

Survivors include his wife, Kalima; sons, Bilal and Mandela; daughters, Jamilah and Zafirah; stepson, Marcus Ball; stepdaughter, Shaunte Ball; his mother, Louise Iverson of Cleveland; and two sisters.

Services will be at 11 a.m. tomorrow at the Rev. Martin Luther King Jr. Civic Center, 14601 Shaw Ave., East Cleveland.

Chapter 16

It's Not Easy Being Grim

ALANA BARANICK

Sometimes I feel like the MTV cartoon character Daria, a cynical teenager who is a fish out of water at her high school, where the popular kids are, for the most part, airheads.

In one "Daria" episode, a rude, self-centered graduate who once quarterbacked the varsity football team dies in an accident. A goalpost falls on him.

Although he had hurt the feelings of everyone with whom he came into contact, the students feel guilty that they don't truly feel sorry that he is gone. One by one, they approach Daria, usually regarded as the outcast, for comfort and counsel. Their reasoning? Daria could advise them because, after all, she is the "Misery Chick."

Colleagues often come talk to the Plain Dealer's Misery Chick when they return to work after the funeral of a loved one. They seem to believe that my death-beat mantle endows me with some kind of divine understanding. But it doesn't.

Reporters in my paper's sports, entertainment and business departments cringe on those occasions when I venture into their sections of the newsroom. They think of me as the Grim Reaper's personal Ed McMahon, ready to announce the latest deaths. They never consider that I might be looking for help with some terminology peculiar to their field.

If a colleague's loved one has been ill, I can't say, "I heard that your mom was in the hospital. How's she doing?" I can see in his eyes the image of me pulling out a tape measure and a notebook, ready to record mom's dimensions for her coffin and her life history for her obit.

Sadly, one of my newsroom friends found it impossible to look me in the eye after he discovered he had the same type of cancer that claimed his late father. I got the impression that he seemed to believe that, if his eyes met mine, he would surrender his grip on life.

I had a similar reaction from another colleague, who was about to retire. I suggested he write his own obit. I didn't mean anything by it. I figure news people should understand the concept of having a story ready in advance, even if it's 20 years in advance. Writers in particular ought to want to get the story right. And who better to do it than they themselves?

My retiring friend was obviously disturbed at my suggestion. I didn't know he had serious health problems. He died a few months later.

When I started writing obits at the Plain Dealer, the old-timers in the newsroom immediately warmed up to me — probably anticipating that I might pen their final chapters. But most of the reporters and editors considered obit writing an entry level position and treated me accordingly.

My longtime colleagues now tell me they appreciate the quality of my work and the difficulties of my job, but newly hired reporters tend to ignore me — until they need my help with a death-related story or are assigned to temporary obit duty.

College interns, younger than my own children, become visibly uneasy and cast sympathetic looks in my direction once they learn that I walk the death beat.

I get the same type of reaction from marketing managers at local night clubs where I used to cover rock bands, and from government officials whom I met while covering various communities for my previous employer. When I have occasion to call them, I am not greeted with the standard, "How've you been?" Instead, the first words to come out of their mouths is, "Who died?"

Say the words "death" or "obituary" to our newsroom telephone operators and chances are your call will be transferred to me.

I've taken calls from amateur geneaologists looking for newspaper reports of relatives who died "sometime between 1902 and 1908." From out-of-towners asking about the location of the funeral for their co-worker's mother. From tipsters who want us to know about a prominent death. From bar patrons, who had a bet riding on when Otis Redding died. From folks wanting to offer their condolences to the deceased's family or get directions to the funeral home.

Others want to share the view as they stroll down Memory Lane, recalling the role the deceased played in their lives. Some want to know whether the artwork the dead craftsman made had increased in value since his death or what his family planned to do with the pieces he left them.

SOME CALLS ARE DEPRESSING. One man told me that he just heard that his brother died a few weeks earlier. He wanted to know if it was true. The two brothers, who had lived most of their lives on opposite sides of the city, apparently hadn't seen or spoken to each other in years.

A woman called from out of state wanting to know whether her father had died in the last year. She had been trying to get in touch with him when someone told her he was dead.

I received an unusually large number of calls from friends of a 34-year-old Persian Gulf War veteran, law student and all-around do-good-er, when they heard that he was killed by a drunk driver.

Then the dead man's mother called to tell me what a great guy he was. She said her son helped school chums overcome drug problems and encouraged friends to pursue their dreams.

I've spoken with other obit writers who often are overcome with emotion while doing their job. That rarely happens to me. But I lost it when that mother told me that her son "brought home stray dogs and stray kids. He was always trying to rescue people. Can you tell me? Why is my son dead?"

Before hanging up the phone and grabbing a box of Kleenex, I did manage to offer a quiet, "I'll let you go now. Thanks for talking to me about your son. Take care of yourself."

When the obituary appeared in print, I received several favorable calls and emails from the dead guy's friends and family, including his mom.

It's always rewarding when bereaved relatives thank us for writing about their loved ones, but we also get our share of complaints. "My father is devastated that you didn't print my mother's obit." "Why didn't you include my dad's dog in the list of surviving relatives?" "You didn't write an obit for my banjo-playing friend, but you wrote one for a 'bleeping' plasterer."

Overall, I love the death beat.

I don't have to pound the pavement in search of a story. My subjects are dying to get in. I don't have to stand in the rain at a crime scene, hoping to get a witness to talk to me. I can stay at my cozy cubicle and conduct interviews over the phone. It's challenging to gather information about a subject who is not available to be interviewed.

Obit writing transcends all newspaper beats. I get to write about people from all walks of life: Politicians and priests, placekickers and playwrights, peddlers and presidents of corporations.

It's Not Easy Being Grim

True, I don't get to go to Hollywood to report on the Oscars; to Winterhaven, Fla. to evaluate the newly-signed outfielder at the Cleveland Indians spring training camp; or to the Middle East or other war-torn locales to see what the combatants and Geraldo Rivera are up to.

Yet I still find excitement on my beat. It just takes a different form.

This is where I have to confess to you. I'm evil. Sometimes the what's-happening-now newsperson, the I-want-to-be-relevant reporter, emerges from deep within me and sticks out its ugly head.

The truth is, I get excited when I get obit information for people whose deaths fall timewise in conjunction with events that are happening in the news. It's not that I'm glad these people are dead. I'm just very pleased with their timing.

Politicians dying on Election Day. War heroes on Veteran's Day. Professional baseball players during the World Series. As Julie Andrews would say, "These are a few of my favorite things." I believe people's lives take on added significance, when their deaths coincide with holidays, special occasions and current events.

On Election Day 2000, while voters were lined up at the polls choosing whether to send then-Vice President Al Gore or then-Texas Governor George W. Bush to the White House, I was notified of the death of a two-term suburban city councilman. His first term was as a Democrat. His second, as a Republican.

I was thrilled to be writing a "bipartisan" obit, which would be printed in the Wednesday edition alongside election results. It got even better. The obituary ran on Nov. 8, 2000, the day after a general election that produced a Senate that was equally divided between Democrats and Republicans and a presidential vote that was too close to call.

Votes for Bush and Gore were still being re-counted in Florida, and the role the Electoral College might play in declaring a winner was becoming a topic of media speculation, when we ran an obit for a presidential elector who cast one of Ohio's 25 electoral votes for Richard M. Nixon in 1960. I was able to work into the obit that Nixon, a Republican, won the state that year by a quarter-million votes over Democrat John F. Kennedy, but lost the popular vote nationally. I also mentioned that the deceased cast an absentee ballot in the 2000 presidential election.

ON CHRISTMAS 1997, we ran an obit for a man whose story provided a yuletide "Twilight Zone" moment.

A couple of weeks before the man's death, his wife went to a second-hand store and purchased a slightly damaged toy church with a wind-up music box that played "Silent Night." After a few days it seemed to be missing.

"We looked everywhere for that thing," said the widow, who later learned that the music box had fallen under her husband's bed.

The night the man died, his family gathered around his bed to pray. In unison, his wife, children and grandchildren recited the Lord's Prayer. As they said "Amen," that church played the last line of the tune: "Sleep in heavenly peace." "Silent Night" was played at the funeral the day after Christmas.

© The Plain Dealer, Aug. 30, 2004

A SPIRIT THAT SOARED WITH THE STARS, ASTROPHYSICIST, 51, FELT A KINSHIP WITH WEST AFRICAN ASTRONOMERS

By Alana Baranick, Plain Dealer Reporter

Willie Ray "Karimi" Mackey felt a kinship with the primitive Dogon people of West Africa, who have been mapping the stars for more than 800 years.

The 51-year-old NASA astrophysicist and African dance instructor was fascinated that the Dogon, who revere Sirius - known as the Dog Star - knew of its tiny companion star, Sirius B, centuries before modern astronomers identified it.

Mackey was pronounced dead, apparently of a heart condition, Aug. 6 - while Sirius was making its annual daytime appearance in the sky.

As a scientist, Mackey conducted far-ranging "fundamental research that doesn't reveal itself until years downstream but is critical to development," said Julian Earls, director of the NASA Glenn Research Center.

But he didn't look like a rocket scientist.

"He had his own style," said NASA colleague Eric Overton. "In appearance, he was so down to earth, you would be shocked to know he even had a job. Then you find out he worked at NASA, had a Ph.D."

Mackey grew up in St. Louis, the eldest of nine children in what was essentially a single-parent household. Ray, as he was known to his family, took care of his younger siblings while his mother worked the midnight shift at the post office. He got them ready for school in the morning and assigned them educational projects after school.

It's Not Easy Being Grim

When his sisters saw a spider in the house, "not only did Ray kill it, he looked it up in the encyclopedia and gave a report," said his sister Karen. "He liked Radio Shack science kits. He outgrew those and started taking things apart in the house. Lamps, appliances. He always found a way to put it back together."

He watched public-television programs like "Nova" to learn about the stars. He tried to instill his passion for the heavens in his siblings and, later, his daughters.

"He made us go in the back yard, and we'd have to look up in the sky," said his sister Yvonne. "He'd say, 'Analyze that.' "

In the early 1970s, Mackey enrolled at Oberlin College, where he and classmate Diaris Jackson were "roaring with ideology, pushing for change, angry that we'd missed the '60s, aware of the special gifts that made us leaders," Jackson said.

Mackey, whose African name, Karimi, means "one whose spirit travels with the stars," went to Boston to study astrophysics at the Massachusetts Institute of Technology. He also trained in African dance and drum under Raymond Sylla, an African cultural icon from Senegal.

After earning a doctorate from MIT in 1981, Mackey taught math at Wilberforce University in southern Ohio. Abasi Ojinjideka, with whom he collaborated on projects integrating cultural arts and science, met him at a Kwanzaa event 22 years ago.

"He was sitting on a drum, listening to music on headphones, reading a book and watching TV at the same time," Ojinjideka said.

Mackey started working for NASA in Brook Park in 1989 but later returned to Wilberforce through a space agency program that allows scientists to spend time at not-for-profit institutions. More recently, NASA lent him to Cheyney University in Pennsylvania.

"We worked together to provide NASA exposure and computer technology for students who lived in a homeless shelter in Philadelphia," said J. Otis Smith, a Cheyney professor. "He was fun to work with. He personally inspired some of our students to overcome their fear of science to explore those fields more closely."

He also did his best to get his twin daughters, Nyonu and Naima, excited about science.

"If you looked in the sky on a clear night, he could tell you the names of the stars," Naima said.

One weekend, while visiting his daughters at Hampton University in Virginia, Mackey woke them at 6:30 a.m., and said, "We're going to Norfolk State University. I want you to see the sunspots in the sky."

When they arrived, "he got out his little sunspot device with a mirror," Naima said. "We saw these little dots that would move across the paper. It was neat."

Chapter 17

Might As Well Face It

Alana Baranick

Sooner or later, death comes to all of us. "There's no way out of it," observes Siggy Marvin, the way-too-serious 12-year-old son of a psychiatrist in the comedy film, "What About Bob?"

As Siggy, actor Charlie Korsmo tells Bob Wiley (Bill Murray), his father's middle-aged patient, "You're going to die. I'm going to die. It's going to happen. And what difference does it make if it's tomorrow or in 80 years? Much sooner in your case."

When death came to my mother in 1998, I realized how difficult it can be for families to put together obituary information, especially when they're dealing with the grief of losing a loved one.

I applaud folks who ask about submitting an obituary before their terminally ill relative dies. I encourage people to write down biographical information about themselves for their own obits. You never know how much your surviving relatives, friends or former employers are going to remember about you after you're gone or how accurate those recollections will be.

Writing Mom's obit was an enlightening experience that left me with more empathy for grieving families seeking obits and more respectful of funeral directors who collect obituary information from them.

Although I knew Mom's death was imminent, my brain had trouble functioning when she finally died. I was scrambling for information. Since she belonged to a cremation society, my sisters and I had to handle most of the duties usually handled by a funeral director. So I was on my own with the obit.

I struggled with listing her surviving relatives. Yes, I knew she had three daughters (myself included) with my father, but there were other kids who came into Mom's life courtesy of two other marriages. She had two stepsons, whom I barely know. How many stepgrandchildren were there, and how should they be listed? And then there's my mother's last husband's nephew, who lived with her since he was in high school. Could we include him as a surviving relative?

The policy for listing surviving relatives and those family members who are dead varies from paper to paper. Realizing that geneaologists sometimes use obits to trace families, some newspapers want to list each marriage, which children came from which spouse or lover and which siblings did not have the same parents. This was not the case at the newspapers where Mom's obit would be submitted.

Although it was unreasonable, I was determined to get my father's name mentioned in Mom's obit. They were divorced more than 40 years before her death, but he was the father of her children. (How many times have I asked bereaved children, "Are you sure your mother would have wanted your father's name in her obit, when she didn't want to be married to him?")

Mom was the last of seven siblings to die. Could we mention all of their names?

Yet with all my concern about things I wanted to include, I was missing some key information. I didn't have dates for when Mom married her last two husbands, when they died, how long she'd lived in Florida or when she retired.

As the bereaved relative contacting Mom's hometown newspaper, I exhibited some of the pretentious behavior that has unnerved or amused me when I — as an obituary writer — have been on the receiving end.

First, I told the obit writer that my late stepfather had been a reporter at his paper, the Beacon in DeLand, Fla. I pointed out that my mother was the widow of that reporter. I added that I too was a reporter, quite capable of composing Mom's story, thank you very much. Then I contacted his boss, who used to work with my stepfather, to make sure the obit writer understood how important my stepfather had been to the community. Never mind that my mother had no other claim to fame there.

I just hate it when obit-seekers drop the names of reporters or the top brass at my paper in hopes of preferential treatment from me. I also get frustrated at folks who tell me they are "journalists," as if we writers belong to some sort of secret brotherhood. Yet I transgressed on both counts. I probably should beg the Florida obit writer for forgiveness.

I should have displayed the class that was demonstrated to me by certain celebrities -- including television's Drew Carey, moviemaker Wes Craven, comedian Don "Father Guido Sarducci" Novello and scriptwriter Joe Eszterhas -- who had a parent die in Greater Cleveland. These celebs could have used their influence to make me write obits for their parents, but they did not.

As for my mom, I wrote an extensive biographical sketch, weaving into it numerous details about her life that would mean nothing to most readers of the DeLand newspaper. Luckily, before faxing it to Florida, I read it to my oldest sister, who saved me from going overboard with a simple observation: "Do you think all of that is necessary?"

Although I trimmed Mom's obit considerably before faxing it to the newspaper, it was still the longest story on the Beacon's obituary page the day it was printed.

Without worrying about newspaper rules, I also penned a short story about Mom — including her flaws and idiosyncracies — for me, my sisters, our kids and great-grandchildren, who would never get to know her. It was more representative of the mother we knew than the obit that was printed in the newspaper.

Nowadays whenever I receive a family-composed obit submission that is particularly touching, well-written or memorable, I recommend that the relatives make copies of it, distribute it to the deceased's loved ones, paste it in their scrapbooks alongside the printed obituary or post it in a paid death notice or on the Internet. Better yet, get other family members and friends to write out their own remembrances of or tributes to the dearly departed and put it in booklet form. Why trust a stranger like me to get it right?

ALTHOUGH I'D LIKE TO PUT OFF MY DEMISE as long as possible, I look at death not as the dreaded consequence of life, but rather as the great transition, the ultimate adventure, the final leg of the journey of a lifetime.

Philosophers, spiritual leaders and dreamers of all kinds have their theories on what we will or will not find once we cross life's border. Yet nobody has been able to produce a reliable road map of the afterlife or even prove that one exists.

What counts is what we do en route to the end quote of our life stories.

Holding down a job, whether it be brain surgery, burger flipping or coal mining, and taking care of our families are significant accomplishments. Not everybody assumes those basic responsibilities.

Often, just keeping our own heads above water can take so much effort that we don't have the time, energy or resources left to breast-stroke across humanity's pond and be effective in offering aid to a fellow swimmer.

We expect clergymen and -women, physicians and employees of social service agencies to be dedicated to helping others. They're paid to do that. But I especially admire people who go beyond these basics, volunteering after their work day is done to help folks who are not their kin.

By writing or reading obituaries, we can discover ways to make our time on earth more worthwhile, more productive, more meaningful to others.

Look in today's newspaper. Chances are you'll read an obit about someone who held a job, took care of family and still had time to help someone else. Learn from that person's example. Be inspired. Go out and make a difference in the world. Do something wonderful for which you'll be remembered. Something that one day might be included in your obituary.

As the "Oz" narrator said: "Ultimately, I guess it don't matter what they write in your obituary, cause you ain't gonna be around to read it. Newsprint fades, paper turns to pulp. The mark you leave behind has to be deeper. The mark you leave behind has to be on another person's soul."

About the Authors

ALANA BARANICK has been writing obituaries for The Plain Dealer in Cleveland, Ohio, since 1992 and loving it. When she won the first of many statewide awards for obit writing, she also won accolades from co-workers who wrote in an in-house newsletter: "The honors only formalized what her colleagues already knew: Alana is one of the best at what she does." The American Society of Newspaper Editors agreed; the group presented her its award for Best News Writing in the obituary category for 2005. The Pittsburgh-area native has been writing for newspapers since 1981, walking the death beat since 1985 and speaking about obit writing to university journalism classes, obit-writers conferences and meetings of professional journalists, funeral directors and civic organizations since 1993. She has two adult sons. She gets her kicks by visiting Clevelands in other states, meeting the locals and picking up stones for her collection of "Cleveland Rocks." Visit her Web site: www.deathbeat.com.

STEPHEN MILLER is an obituaries editor for the New York Sun in Manhattan. He formerly worked as a technologist for a bank located in the World Trade Center, escaping from the 80th floor of the south tower on 9/11. He subsequently decided to pursue a career in writing instead of financial technology. He also has done graduate work in anthropology, and worked as a reporter at newspapers in the New York metropolitan area. He lives in Brooklyn with his wife and young son, who are cheerful reminders that not all the important people in his life are dead.

JIM SHEELER has written obituaries regularly since 1996, when he began his narrative obituary features of everyday people for the Boulder Planet. In 1998 he began a weekly feature called "A Colorado Life" in the Denver Post, which he continued to write for the next four years. Now a general assignment reporter with the Rocky Mountain News in Denver, he has won more than 50 awards from professional groups including the Colorado Society of Professional Journalists, Colorado Associated Press Editors and Reporters, and Best of the West. His work has also appeared in the Houston Chronicle, the Philadelphia Inquirer, and the Dallas Morning News. Sheeler was born and raised in Texas and moved to Colorado in 1986 to attend Colorado State University. He has since logged thousands of miles throughout his adopted state in search of Colorado lives. An anthology of his obituaries will be published in 2005 by Pruett Publishing. For information, access jimsheeler.com.

Index